National Health Insurance in Canada and Australia

A Comparative Political Economy Analysis

Health Economics Research Unit

National Health Insurance in Canada and Australia

Research Monograph 3

A Comparative Political Economy Analysis

Malcolm C. Brown

The Australian National University, Canberra
Health Economics Research Unit
in association with the Centre for
Research on Federal Financial Relations

First published in Australia 1983

Printed in Australia for the Health Economics Research Unit
and by the Australian National University Printing Service.

Health Economics Research Unit 1983

National Library of Australia
Cataloguing-in-Publication entry

Brown, Malcolm C. (Malcolm Clarence), 1941- .
  National health insurance in Canada and Australia.

  ISBN 0 86784 281 4

  1. Insurance, Health - Australia. 2. Insurance,
  Health - Canada. I. Australian National University.
  Health Economics Research Unit. II. Title.
  (Series : Research Monograph (Australian National
  University. Health Economics Research Unit); no. 3).

368.4'2'00994

CONTENTS

LIST OF TABLES

ACKNOWLEDGEMENTS

This monograph is a product of work done while I was on sabbatical leave from the University of Calgary, Alberta, Canada, during 1982-83; and while I was at the Australian National University as a Visiting Fellow, simultaneously at the Health Economics Research Unit and at the Centre for Research on Federal Financial Relations. Accordingly, I must thank the University of Calgary, the Health Economics Research Unit and the Centre for Research on Federal Financial Relations, without whose collective help this monograph would not have been physically possible.

With respect to financial support, a major vote of thanks must go to the Social Sciences and Humanities Research Council of Canada, which provided me both with a Sabbatical Leave Fellowship (No. 451-82-2834) and with a Research Grant (No. 410-82-0005).

With respect to academic and professional advice, a number of people must be mentioned. Discussions with, and comments by, Professor Russell Mathews, Dr. Dick Scotton, Dr. Michael Tatchell and Dr. Thelma Hunter on the subject matter under consideration were all helpful. But the major contributor in this regard was Dr. John Deeble, who spent an endless amount of time explaining the dynamics of Australian health policy to me, and who occasionally nudged my discussion and analysis in directions which it might otherwise not have gone. In expressing my thanks to these individuals, I of course do not wish to burden them with the views expressed in the monograph. They remain my responsibility alone.

Finally, but far from least importantly, I must thank my wife, Burdette, who, among other things, typed numerous drafts of the manuscript both cheerfully and without pay. My work resulted in demands on her time and energy which it was sometimes easy to overlook, because of the automatic way in which she accepted the responsibilities and commitments involved.

CHAPTER 1

INTRODUCTION

As the title implies, the objective of this monograph is to analyse the evolution of health insurance policy in Canada and Australia. The study is in part motivated by the fact that, while most economic studies suggest that public health insurance is both more efficient and more equitable than private insurance, at a political level there remains strong opposition to it. A comparative study of health financing arrangements is one way of gleaning some insights about why and how this is the case.

While the above paragraph explains what the objective of the study is, it does not explain why particular attention is directed to the health insurance arrangements in Canada and Australia. In this regard, there are obvious advantages in comparing countries which are similar in their social, cultural and economic features. Thus the comparability of Canada and Australia with respect to geographic size, population distribution, economic development, federal political structure, and Anglo-Saxon cultural tradition makes them logical choices for a comparative analysis in almost any context. In the case of national health insurance, there is an important additional consideration. In 1975, Australia introduced a national health insurance system (called Medibank) which was modelled on Canada's hospital and medical insurance programs. Medibank was subsequently dismantled at an extremely rapid rate between 1976 and 1982. Why these programs have been viable in Canada, at least to date, and not in Australia, is a question which provides a very convenient focus for considering the political economy forces which arise in relation to national health insurance.

The monograph is organized as follows. The rest of this chapter is devoted to considering the analytical aspects of national health insurance. Chapter 2 discusses the evolution of health financing arrangements in the context of advances in medical technology. The discussion embraces not only Canada and Australia but also Britain and the United States (the two countries from which Canada and Australia have imported most of their health care practices and traditions). Chapter 3 discusses the history of health insurance policy in Canada, and Chapter 4 discusses it in Australia. The last chapter - Chapter 5 - draws out the inter-country health policy comparisons that can be made, and considers the insights which they provide.

The Objectives of National Health Insurance

Although economists are understandably extremely interested in the efficiency and equity characteristics of national health insurance, political decisions to either implement or reject such systems are generally based on non-economic criteria. Indeed the major reason for introducing national health insurance usually is to substantially reduce, if not completely eliminate, patient user charges in respect of most hospital and medical services. This objective is based on a social philosophy which deems health services to be necessities, the consumption of which should not be constrained by the ability to pay.

Reducing patient charges was clearly the major reason for introducing national health insurance in Canada (in 1958 and 1968) and in Australia (in 1975). However, there were also two other reasons common to both countries. First, there was a desire to give the federal government more power in the health care field than was provided for in the constitution. While the justification for this was never clearly stated, the objective seems to have been based on a view that health standards in an advanced country must, to a substantial degree, be a national concern. The Canadian and Australian constitutions, which implied otherwise, were considered by proponents of this view to be outmoded, reflecting health conditions of fifty to one hundred years ago. Second, there was a desire to replace private insurance with public insurance. While ideological considerations may have played a minor role in formulating this objective, particularly in Australia, its basic justification was administrative. Policymakers in both Canada and Australia understood intuitively that it was easier to constrain budgets of public agencies than it was to regulate costs of private firms.

The Efficiency Characteristics of National Health Insurance

The explicit social and political objectives of national health insurance play an important role in defining both support for and opposition to it. For example, in both Canada and Australia, there has been a certain amount of opposition to national health insurance on the basis of its "socializing" and "centralizing" features - features disliked by conservative members and groups of society. In this milieu, it is often difficult to tell what kind of role economic considerations play - not least because the economic impact of national health insurance arrangements is not widely understood (and, indeed, in many instances, is actually misunderstood).

A major problem of private enterprise medicine, well recognized by economists but barely appreciated by society, is that it invariably involves doctor controlled rather than competitive markets. [1] This control is conducive to prices which are too high and to outputs which are too low from the perspective of economic efficiency. The inefficiency problem is exacerbated by the existence of any kind of insurance arrangement which leaves doctors in control over fees. At the limit, such insurance becomes a mechanism for increasing doctors' incomes while frustrating

---

[1]

The following publications all discuss some of the economic problems resulting from doctor controlled health care markets: Brown (1974), Dodge (1972), Kessel (1958) and Lees (1966).

[3]

patients' efforts to buy protection from financial contingencies associated with illness. For this reason, most kinds of private insurance arrangements combined with doctor controlled markets tend to represent the worst of all possible economic worlds, as far as patients and consumers are concerned.

One way (although clearly not the only way) of alleviating the problem of physician control is by the creation of a national health insurance system. Nationalization of the insurance function is conducive to governments, or their agencies, bargaining with medical associations over fees. Since governments have a considerable amount of monopsony power in this regard, they have considerable capacity for offsetting the monopoly pricing practices of the medical profession. And even if governments are not overly inclined to exercise this power, it is doubtful that their bargaining could lead to worse pricing results than does that of patient-consumers, who have no power at all.

However, there is a way of inducing governments to bargain vigorously over prices, and that is by setting up a national health insurance system which involves zero user charges. If governments do not bargain vigorously in such an arrangement, medical fees have a propensity to spiral upwards at an increasing rate as doctors become more aggressive in their income demands. In effect, because of the instability of the underlying market arrangement, governments have to constrain doctors' demands at some point, and it might as well be sooner as later. On the other hand, if the public payments constitute only a portion of the fees, then it is possible for governments to let the market define an equilibrium. This lets governments which dislike the political problems associated with bargaining off the hook, but results in prices which are high even by monopoly standards. [2]

There is ample evidence that the implementation of national health insurance constrains health costs, as theoretical considerations suggest. Consider the evidence concerning Canada, which completely phased in its national health insurance system about 1970. After that point, the growth rate in health costs dropped dramatically (Table 1-1). In constant dollar terms, hospital operating expenditures grew by approximately 11 percent annually before 1970, and 8 percent annually after that. The comparable growth rates for medical services were 9 percent and 6 percent. On the face of it, national health insurance in Canada had the effect of reducing the growth rate in health care costs by about 3 percentage points.

The causal relationship between the introduction of national health insurance in Canada and the reduction in the growth rate in health costs might be disputed, were it not for the fact that the Canadian experience fits into a pattern exhibited by most countries. R.E. Leu, who examined this pattern by doing a multiple regression study on the determinants of health care expenditures across countries, came to the following conclusion:

> "Both public supply and public financing seem to increase health care costs. There is, however, an exception: health services systems that are highly centralized appear to operate at lowest costs" (1980, pp.162-163).

As explained earlier, the lower costs are obtained in part by constraining the fee demands of medical practitioners. However, the data in Table 1-1 make it clear that they are also obtained through relatively stringent budgeting procedures for hospitals. In both cases, the motivating force tends to be the same. Since governments under national health insurance arrangements are responsible for most costs, they must take an active interest in controlling them. In contrast, under private arrangements where costs are distributed

---

2

It is often pointed out that reducing user charges to zero creates inefficiency by inducing patients to over-consume. However, the argument is not as clear cut as it might be because national health insurance is invariably opted for where private insurance is common but found to be inadequate. Moreover, it is difficult in principle to assess the welfare implications of individuals voluntarily voting to supplant the market, particularly if it is assumed that they understand the economic implications of their action. Finally, it is not clear that patients have much control over their consumption of health care services.

Table 1-1: Expenditure on Medical Care and on Services of General and Allied Special Hospitals in Canada (1961 Dollars)

Year	Medical Care		Hospital Care	
	$000	Average Annual Growth Rate (%)	$000	Average Annual Growth Rate (%)
1955	230,212		381,717	
1960	359,326	9.31	639,278	10.86
1965	506,558	7.11	1,048,027	10.39
1970	794,115	9.40	1,746,383	10.75
1975	1,041,931	5.58	2,588,002	8.18

Sources: (1) Health and Welfare Canada (1961).

(2) Health and Welfare Canada (1978).

Note: The data are deflated by means of the consumer price index.

among patients, charities, private insurers and governments, no one funding unit (including governments) has reason to be concerned.

The above discussion is not meant to leave the impression that cost containment and economic efficiency are necessarily synonymous. Cost containment can be achieved in economically inefficient ways, such as by letting capital become obsolete or by phasing out socially beneficial programs. Despite the tenuous link between cost containment and efficiency, the potential of national health schemes for true economies makes them extremely attractive. It was part of the reason why Australian policymakers during the early 1970's were attracted by the Canadian health financing arrangements.

Finally, it should be noted that there is another efficiency reason for favouring public health insurance over private health insurance, other than the lack of competition in the private sector. Because of the nature of market pressures, private insurers must always allocate resources to identifying and attracting low risk insurees. In a system where most citizens are expected to be insured, and at adequate levels of coverage, this resource allocation is wasteful. A single public insurer, not operating on a profit maximizing basis, would not have any incentive to allocate funds in this way.

The empirical evidence supports the theoretical deduction that public insurers should have lower administrative costs than their private counterparts. Canadian studies done both in the mid-1950's and in the mid-1960's established that the public health insurance plans in Saskatchewan and British Columbia, whether for hospital and/or medical services, had premium collections and/or tax revenues equal to about 105 percent of benefits paid out to patients (see Taylor, 1978, p.114; and LeClair, 1975, p.16). The corresponding ratio for Blue Cross in Ontario was 118 percent (ibid.). Commercial group insurance plans achieved a ratio of 130 percent while commercial individual insurance topped the list at 170 percent (ibid.). Even the co-operatives achieved the relatively high ratio of 116 percent (ibid.).

The Australian evidence on private health insurance costs, collected in the late 1960's, fits into the Canadian pattern in a consistent way. The most common expense rates were 11 to 13 percent for hospital funds and 14 to 16 percent for medical funds (Committee of Inquiry into Health Insurance, 1969, p.45).

The Equity Characteristics of National Health Insurance

Equity is a more difficult issue to discuss than efficiency, because of the necessity for making some explicit value judgements in order to develop operational criteria for the evaluation of policy. There are two major value judgements incorporated into the subsequent discussion. The first is that a social policy which has equalizing inter-personal income transfers is, other things being equal, superior to one that does not. The second is that, the larger the proportion of a population that favours a particular social policy, the greater is the equity rationale for implementing it.

Although national health insurance is basically an income equalizing social program, it is important to note that the equalizing effect is relatively small when income is measured on a lifetime (or permanent) basis. At any point in time, national health insurance transfers income from the healthy to the sick. But over a lifetime, most people fit into both categories. Thus much of the inter-personal income transfer implicit in national health insurance is self-reversing over time. Consequently, for most middle income people, national health insurance has extremely minor implications with respect to inter-personal income transfers. There remain, of course, adverse income transfer implications for a small proportion of the population that is extremely rich. But even they might still favour national health insurance, depending on how they perceive the effects of the "Robin Hood" pricing practices commonly adopted by doctors in private marketing arrangements. Finally, for the very poor, there are no negative implications of national health

[8]

insurance. Not only does it provide them with protection against financial contingencies associated with illness, but also it transfers permanent income to themselves from others.

The income transfer implications of national health insurance imply that it should be popular with most people - and consumer surveys tend to support the validity of this view. The Canadian surveys are instructive. A gallup poll conducted in 1944, and another conducted in 1949, established that 80 percent of the population supported the idea of introducing a national health program (Taylor, 1978, p.166). A much more recent study, done in 1980, indicated that support for the principle of medicare remained high, even in very conservative parts of the country (Northcott, 1982). But the same survey also indicated that, when the national health insurance principle broke down through physician private billing, consumers tended to blame governments rather than doctors. In the words of the author of the survey, the responses supported the suggestion:

> "that there (was) strong public opposition to the practice of extra-billing .... it may seem paradoxical that the public strongly opposes extra-billing while at the same time supporting continued high levels of physician remuneration .... it seems that the public's opposition is against the mechanism of extra-billing as a means of generating physician income and not against the high level of physician income .... the public endorses the concept of 'adequate compensation' and defines 'adequate' as a rate of increase in line with the general rate of income rise and in line with the rate of inflation" (ibid., p.206).

Even in the United States, which has never had a national health insurance program, there is evidence of electoral support for such a system. Opinion surveys from 1943 to 1965 indicated that about two-thirds of Americans favoured government assistance in the financing of health services (Marmor, 1970, p.3). However, most people were unsure about the optimal form which this assistance should take - thus leaving governments the option of meeting electoral demands by subsidizing parts of the private sector.

[9]

The Australian consumer surveys, like those in the United States, are hard to interpret concerning their implications for the amount of support for national health insurance. When Australians were asked to choose between compulsory health insurance and voluntary health insurance in 1963, 45 percent chose compulsory insurance, 53 percent chose voluntary insurance, and 2 percent were undecided (Gray, 1982, p.50). By 1969, the respective percentages were 58, 39, and 3; and by 1976, they were 46, 35, and 19 (ibid.). One problem with interpreting these numbers is that compulsory insurance is not synonymous with public comprehensive insurance; and, voluntary insurance is not synonymous with private insurance; although it is probable that, in the Australian context, most people thought so. A more serious problem is that, in the Australian context, it was reasonable for people to associate both compulsory insurance and voluntary insurance with a substantial amount of direct governmental funding. What the surveys were measuring, therefore, is not clear.

Concluding Remarks

Despite the difficulties that invariably exist in interpreting social statistics, it seems fair to say that national health insurance arrangements tend to be both relatively efficient, and popular with electorates. On the basis of such evidence, one might expect national health insurance to be a relatively common method of health funding. Yet a country like the United States has never managed a national health insurance system, and a country like Australia installed one only to dismantle it almost immediately. Since these developments appear inexplicable at an analytical level, an alternative kind of approach must be adopted to identify the factors that are conducive to the implementation and maintenance of viable national health insurance systems.

CHAPTER 2

THE TECHNOLOGICAL AND HISTORICAL BACKDROP TO MODERN HEALTH DELIVERY SYSTEMS

A basic justification for making comparative studies of Canada and Australia is the general similarity in the evolution and status of their socio-economic systems. Both countries originally developed as a number of separate colonies of Great Britain, eventually joining to become federal states. While both countries were originally heavily influenced by Britain in cultural and institutional matters, the influence of Britain has waned while that of the United States has waxed over time. Today, both Canada and Australia have highly developed and affluent economies, and both are geographically large countries with small and widely dispersed populations.

The similarities between Canada and Australia are reflected not only at the macroeconomic level but also with respect to many individual sectors of the economy. The early evolution of technology and institutions in the health field, for example, are remarkably similar between the two countries. It is useful to sketch out some of those similarities, not only for the purpose of defining the common base from which divergencies in health care policies and practices can be evaluated, but also as a convenient way of considering some of the basic relationships between health technology and health economics.

The Evolution of Health Technology

While some sort of approach to illness and disease has existed during the entirety of man's history, most medical histories tend to start with the contribution of Hippocrates in Corpus Hippocraticum, a collection of treatises written in Greece during the fifth century B.C. [3] Hippocrates' great service to medicine was that of eliminating the supernatural from health care, and replacing it with a naturalistic approach. He also developed a creed of medical ethics which is paid lip service to even today.

Despite the complexity of medical history it is possible to identify four major periods - classical medicine, which ran from about 500 B.C. to 500 A.D.; medieval medicine, which ran from 500 A.D. to about 1500 A.D.; renaissance medicine, which lasted until 1865; and modern medicine, which has continued up to the present. As mentioned in the foregoing paragraph, the classical period represented the first time in man's history that a naturalistic approach to disease was adopted. Hippocrates' cures consisted mostly of rest, good food, fresh air and sanitary conditions. Medieval medicine, which followed the classical period, was initiated by the fall of Rome. During this period the standard of medical care declined. The practice of medicine was taken over by clerics who augmented the naturalistic approach with procedures like purges and bloodletting, based on the Church's notion that illness was a punishment for sin. During the second half of the medieval period, university trained doctors took over from the clerics, but this was not to have a significant effect on either the standard or character of medical practice until the renaissance period. [4] Even then, the effect of secularization on medicine occurred in a rather peculiar way. During the renaissance years the emphasis shifted from "theoretical" medicine to "practical" medicine. While physicians retained a university education as a part of their training, they augmented it heavily with an apprenticeship program for the learning of bedside skills. Surgery also developed extensively during this period, because of the discovery of gunpowder which led to a

---

[3]

Interestingly enough, many of the treatises were written not by Hippocrates himself, but by his students and followers.

[4]

It was the university trained practitioners who adopted the title of doctor, suggesting that initially the title indicated that a person had a university degree rather than that he was a medical practitioner.

substantial increase in the number of serious wounds. [5] Initially, surgeons received all of their training through apprenticeship, since it was regarded as a manual skill not requiring a formal education. However, neither physicians nor surgeons had a general understanding of the causes of illness. This was not to develop until the period of modern medicine, with the advent of the germ theory of disease.

The length of histories on medical science and the documentation of important biological discoveries (like William Harvey's discovery of the mechanical process of blood circulation in 1628) give the impression that doctors since Hippocrates have had significant technical expertise to help patients. Nothing could be further from the truth. Until well into the twentieth century doctors, at best, were relatively ineffective in dealing with most illnesses and, at worst, interfered with patients' natural capacities for recovery. Ironically, Hippocrates, who is usually reputed to have been the first doctor, was undoubtedly one of the best until at least late in the nineteenth century. His naturalistic cures were much better than the orthodox therapeutic procedures of bloodletting, purging, induced vomiting, and large doses of toxic drugs common between 1650 and 1850 (Ackerknecht, 1955, p.131). It is of note that William Harvey, even after his discovery of the principle of blood circulation, continued to engage in bloodletting, suggesting a significant split between his scientific work and his medical practice. [6]

Until the middle of the nineteenth century the standard of health, as measured by the few indicators available, remained largely static. The major causes of death besides war were the epidemic diseases - smallpox, yellow fever, bubonic plague, dysentery and

---

[5]

The first well-known surgeon was Pare (1510-1590) who became famous for his work on gunshot wounds (Ackerknecht, 1955, p.100).

[6]

For a general analysis of the split between medical knowledge and practice see Jewson (1974).

cholera, to name some of the more important - and these were diseases that medical practitioners could not cope with. Reducing mortality rates from these diseases was only possible when an understanding of their contagious nature was achieved.

Louis Pasteur was the man most responsible for creating this understanding. He revived interest in the germ theory of disease, first by establishing that beer and wine fermentation is caused by bacteria, and later by establishing that silkworm disease is caused by the same kinds of organisms (1865). [7] Pasteur correctly deduced that what was true of one infectious disease (the silkworm disease) was probably true of most others. [8]

Effectively Pasteur's work initiated the era of modern medicine, which can be conveniently separated into four periods - 1865 through 1900 when many conceptual advances relating to the germ theory occurred, 1900 through 1921 when many significant improvements in public health policies were implemented, 1921 through 1967 when many effective curative health procedures involving drugs were discovered, and 1967 to the present when society has become aware of the fact that the major health problems facing mankind involve the degenerative illnesses of heart disease and cancer. [9]

From 1865 to the beginning of the twentieth century most of the medical work related to the identification of the various bacteria

---

[7]

Contrary to popular opinion Louis Pasteur was not the first person to develop the germ theory of disease.

[8]

See Asimov (1965) for a discussion of Pasteur's work.

[9]

From the perspective of the evolution of medical technology, 1967 is an arbitrary date, based on the fact that this was the year the national health insurance was originally intended to be fully implemented in Canada. The disillusionment with medical technology, referred to in the text, became more and more in evidence during the late 1960's and early 1970's. In this context, it is spuriously accurate to assert that it started in 1967. Similarly, the other dates mentioned in the text - 1865, 1900 and 1921 - all have a degree of spuriousness to them.

and to the discovery of their transmission mechanisms. In 1880 Charles Laveran established that malaria is spread through bites of infected mosquitos, in 1882 Robert Koch identified the tuberculosis bacterium, in 1894 the diptheria antitoxin was developed, and in 1902 Charles Nicolle established that lice can spread typhoid fever. Discoveries of this nature fostered a much better understanding of the infectious nature of many diseases, and paved the way for great strides in public health policies during the first two decades of the twentieth century.

During the first two decades of the twentieth century, vaccination programs were greatly extended, pasteurization of milk was developed, substantial improvements in garbage and water systems were made, and the health delivery system became more concerned about the maintenance of sanitary conditions in hospitals and other institutions. [10] Man had learned how to avoid many diseases, if not how to alleviate them in process. The effects of these improvements is reflected in the Montreal death rate per 1,000 population, which declined from 25.5 in 1900 to 17.2 in 1921. [11]

During the mid-part of the twentieth century, with the discovery of the wonder drugs, curative health care came of age. I have dated the beginning of this period as 1921, when Banting discovered insulin, although obviously the discovery of the sulfonamides in the late 1930's, and penicillin and streptomycin a few years later, were in many ways more important.

The above dating of the modern era is, of course, more influenced by developments concerning pharmaceutical medicine than by advances in surgery. In fact, surgical practice benefited far more quickly from the development of the germ theory than did medicine. It must be

---

[10]
  See Heagerty (1928) for an extensive discussion of public health problems and policies in Canada prior to 1925.

[11]
  The death rates in the text are crude death rates, not standardized for the age structure of the population (Urquhart and Buckley, 1965, p.43).

recalled that before 1865 most surgical patients died from shock and/or infection. The problem of shock was actually resolved somewhat before 1865, anaesthetics being introduced into both Canada and Australia in 1847 (Heagerty, 1928, p.273; and Pensabene, 1980, p.34). The problem of infection was resolved in 1867 with Joseph Lister's discovery of antiseptic methods (Ackerknecht, 1955, p.173). Antiseptic procedures were introduced into Canada and Australia during the 1870's, and their value was beyond dispute. Of 10 operations done in Ontario without carbolic sprays during the early 1870's, 8 were fatal. The introduction of sprays later in the decade reduced the death rate for similar sorts of operations to 2 in 64 (MacDermot, 1967, p.29).

The fact that technological advance favoured surgery over pharmaceutical medicine had a significant impact on the evolution of health delivery systems. Particularly in the United States, the surgical specialist was able to obtain and hold a more prestigious position, both professionally and socially, than was his medical counterpart. Because of the historical success of surgical methods there was a tendency to favour them over pharmaceutical methods, where technology allowed a choice. Correspondingly, there was a tendency to emphasize the use of hospital facilities over home care, because surgery was a hospital oriented activity.

It must not be inferred from the above discussion that medical developments after 1865 proceeded in a completely rational way. A particularly objectionable trend during this period was the development of routine surgery on healthy organs. Agnew recollects how, during his internship at the University of Toronto in the early 1920's, he was required to assist an otolaryngologist with 12 tonsillectomies during a morning's work. While helping, Agnew confessed that he had not had his own tonsils removed. Immediate arrangements were made for an extra operation, with some joking about his being the thirteenth patient (Agnew, 1974). While such surgery is currently viewed as excessive, the practitioners of the time obviously believed in its efficacy.

Not all of the medical practitioner procedures during the 1865 to 1930 period can be defended on the basis of misguided evaluation of the benefits from medical therapies, however. For example, as late as the 1920's when there was almost universal acceptance of the germ theory, many doctors refused to wear gloves in surgery, and made little effort to prevent perspiration from falling on open incisions (ibid., p.16).

Despite lapses in attention to the implications of the germ theory, its general acceptance facilitated improvements in health programs hitherto impossible not only for technological reasons but also for social reasons. It is of particular note that vaccination did not become widespread until the germ theory was generally accepted, even though it had been discovered by Edward Jenner in 1798. As long as antagonism to the germ theory remained strong, many people refused to be vaccinated. Among French Canadians, for example, this antagonism extended well into the twentieth century when, in 1921, there was a smallpox epidemic in Ottawa killing 1,352 people (Heagerty, 1928).

The last period of the modern era dates from 1967, when a growing belief has been emerging that society has reaped most of the benefits available from appreciation of the germ theory of disease. Medical clinicians and researchers have increasingly had to turn their attention to the major degenerative diseases (most notably heart disease and cancer), where the available evidence suggests that the most immediate problems stem from life style and environment. In part because of the health delivery system's inability to deal with these problems, this most recent period has been characterised by a growing scepticism about the benefits flowing from the huge sums of money allocated to health care. But it is convenient to leave the discussion on this matter to the last section of this chapter, after the history of institutional developments concerning health care has been considered.

The History of Medical Practice

It is interesting that, from the beginning of European medical history, surgical practice has tended to be separated from medical practice, although it has only been in the modern era that surgeons have been accorded more respect than physicians. From the early days of Greece to the middle of the nineteenth century, medicine was viewed as the profession of gentlemen while surgery was regarded as basically a manual skill. Accordingly, surgery was generally left to the labouring classes (mainly barbers during the renaissance period because they possessed useful cutting tools). In the Middle Ages the tradition was accentuated by giving physicians long and expensive liberal arts educations, while surgeons were confined to the practical knowledge learned through apprenticeship. It is a matter of interest that the surgeon-barber combination remained until 1731 in France, at which time the Royal Academy of Surgery was founded, and until 1745 in England (Ackerknecht, 1955, p.118; and Jewson, 1974, p.374). The tradition of addressing surgeons as "Mr" has been maintained in Britain to the present time, resulting from the origins of the profession.

By the eighteenth century there were actually three types or classes of doctors in Britain - physicians, surgeons and apothecaries. The physicians were the most prestigious, and the fewest in number. The cost of their education at places like Oxford and Cambridge was long and expensive, and kept all but the wealthy out of the profession (ibid.). The apothecaries, on the other hand, were the least prestigious, and the most numerous (ibid.). After 1703 they had the right to practise medicine, but could only charge for the drugs they prescribed (ibid.). The apothecaries were required to call upon the physician in serious cases, thus laying the basis for the practice of consultation (ibid.).

While, by the beginning of the nineteenth century, physicians and surgeons had hospital appointments and belonged to Royal Colleges, the apothecaries did not (Sax, 1972, p.39). The apothecaries gradually evolved into general practitioners, forming the British Medical Association in 1855 (ibid.). The evolution of the British profession led to a system involving general practitioners as privately employed and non-hospital based professionals, and physicians and surgeons as salaried and hospital based medical specialists.

The social differentiation between physicians and surgeons common in Europe prior to 1865 never existed to the same degree in the United States, Canada or Australia. In part, this was because the colonies developed more egalitarian philosophies than had their homelands, particularly in their early development stages. But the more significant factor was that all colonies received mostly surgeons, and very few physicians, as settlers and immigrants. This was the case primarily because most European nations required surgeons on their sailing ships, but it was also the case that surgeons, with their lower social and economic status than physicians, had more to gain through migration (Ackerknecht, 1955, p.205; and Heagerty, 1928, p.223). As the only practitioners in the colonies, surgeons tended to provide all aspects of medical care.

The preponderance of surgeons in the colonies contributed to some significant differences in medical practice from what existed in Europe, particularly after 1865 when surgical technology initially advanced much more rapidly than medical and pharmaceutical technology. The surgeon became a driving force for the development of the hospital sector, and for the substitution of institutional care for ambulatory care. The relatively extreme developments along these lines, particularly in the United States, but also in Canada and Australia, to this day is a major factor conducive to high costs in these countries' health delivery systems.

Development of the Hospital Sector

In a technological sense, the history of hospitals really starts somewhere late in the nineteenth century. This does not imply an absence of institutions called hospitals before this time. But in a technical sense the major medical problem up to at least the beginning of the twentieth century (and really beyond) was infectious disease. This was a problem hospital patients exposed themselves more to than did the general population. Paul Starr makes the following comment about nineteenth century American hospitals:

> "If the demand for physician services was relatively low, the demand for hospital services was still lower. Almost no one who had a choice sought hospital care; there was no market in it. Hospitals were regarded with dread and rightly so. They were dangerous places; when sick, people were safer at home" (1977, p.592).

In Europe, hospitals had their inception in 1145 A.D., with the spread of the Holy Ghost hospitals from Montpelier (Ackerknecht, 1955, p.85). These early Christian organizations were primarily philanthropic in purpose, set up to offer refuge and aid to the old, the poor and the sick, rather than to alleviate disease. This orientation remained until the beginning of the twentieth century.

Because of their orientation, the number of hospitals increased rapidly during the Industrial Revolution when urbanization displaced a great many people (ibid., p.134). England, during the first half of the nineteenth century, developed three classes of hospitals - municipal hospitals to look after parishes' statutory poor (paupers), voluntary hospitals to look after the deserving poor (workers made destitute through accidents and illness), and private hospitals to care for the rich. The municipal hospitals, which were to become the British public hospitals in the twentieth century, were tax financed. The voluntary hospitals received most of their money from gifts and donations from the gentry. Finally, the private hospitals were financed through patient charges (Anderson, 1972, p.46).

While the municipal hospitals very early developed a tradition of tax finance and salaried doctors, the voluntary and private hospitals evolved differently. Not only did they obtain the bulk of their revenues from private sources, but more significantly they developed a tradition of obtaining doctors' services indirectly.

The doctors who worked in these hospitals charged wealthy patients fees (which were independent of the hospital charges), and provided services for poor patients free.

It is significant that the private hospital was the major type of hospital to develop in the United States during the nineteenth entury. In part, this was because the United States did not have any equivalent to the British enclosure movement, which created a large body of unemployed and displaced people. Since unemployment and poverty were not the problems in America that they were in Britain, philanthropic objectives played a lesser role in the evolution of hospital finance. A second factor explaining the late nineteenth century development of the American hospital sector was the tradition of most doctors serving as both surgeons and general practitioners. This required a health delivery system in which hospital practice and private practice were compatible, rather than mutually exclusive, activities. In this context, American doctors showed a marked preference for working in hospitals via "access rights".

In Britain, in contrast to the United States, the charitable work of private medical practitioners became more onerous as the nineteenth century progressed. For this reason, they pressed the government to assume most, if not all, of the financing responsibility for poor patients. This ultimately resulted in the National Health Insurance Act 1911, under which the Government agreed to pay private practitioners a fixed amount per year for each person given free care. This kind of financing system, under which the doctor's annual per capita payment was independent of how much care he provided, became known as capitation.

The nineteenth century British voluntary and private hospitals in most respects were more comparable to modern day nursing homes than to modern day hospitals. Largely because of the inadequacy of pharmaceutical therapies, many diseases like tuberculosis could only be treated on a bed rest and intensive nursing care basis.

However, while the poor and moderately wealthy used hospitals for recuperating from such diseases, the rich insisted on home care. It was the care of the rich which the entrepreneurially minded private practitioners were primarily geared up for. However, this gave them a problem when technological advances made hospital care much more important during the first part of the twentieth century. British private practitioners, in contrast to their American counterparts, were eliminated from the hospital sector almost completely during this period. By 1920, the options of the average British GP were to work in a health centre on salary, or in a surgery (private office) on a combination of capitation (for the poor) and fee-for-service (for everyone else). Most opted for the latter. British specialists, whether physicians or surgeons, tended to become hospital based salaried employees.

Thus, by the early 1920's, the period of modern medical technology had arrived, and two basic funding models had evolved for its finance. There was the British, or European model, which encompassed any health delivery system in which the payment arrangement separated institutional (primarily hospital) services from ambulatory (primary GP) care. And there was the American model, which separated the finance of doctors' services from those of all other health workers. The Canadian and Australian health financing arrangements drew from these two models although, not surprisingly, the Canadian system was relatively more influenced by the American model while the Australian system was more influenced by the British.

The Golden Age of Medicine

From the perspective of doctors in North America, and to a degree elsewhere as well, the 1920's ushered in a golden age of medicine. Medical technology had finally improved to the extent that doctors could alleviate many diseases already in progress. The general public became increasingly aware of this and bestowed on the doctor an even more elevated social status than he had had traditionally. In addition to elevated social status, society gave to medical practitioners great economic power to regulate their markets. Not only were they allowed to limit entry into their ranks, but also they were able to press for social capital, like hospitals, which increased medical incomes, without appearing greedy and in opposition to the public interest.

Of course, the golden age also created problems as far as doctors were concerned. The high value which society placed on medical services meant that pressures developed for more services and lower prices. In policy terms this meant either a more competitive supply of doctors or socialized medicine, either of which would destroy the golden age.

In no country has the competitive option ever won out, although discussions in the United States at times give the impression that it has. The reality, however, is that the American Medical Association and other medical groups retain significant control over physician manpower conditions, hospital management arrangements, and most other health care matters bearing on the financial welfare of doctors. Thus, from the perspective of control, the golden age of medicine in the United States is still alive and well. From the perspective of medical technology, however, the assessment must be qualified. The growing disillusionment with the effectiveness of physician and hospital services over the last decade has been conducive to a drop in the social prestige of doctors, and to an increasing perception that many of them are over-paid. While this has not led to any major changes in American public policy as yet, it is conducive to both redefining and diminishing the role and importance of doctors in the health delivery system.

In Britain, the option of socialized medicine was chosen. Thus it might be argued that Britain's golden age ended in 1948, with the implementation of the National Health Services Act. Among other things, the Act required private practice doctors to accept all patients (and not just the poor as had been the case since 1911) on the basis of capitation - with the government tax financing the premiums.

In an earlier paper, I suggested that Canada's golden age of medicine lasted from 1921 to 1967 (Brown, 1979). The choice of 1921 was based on three considerations - it was the year that Banting discovered insulin in Toronto, it was just after the period when Canadian governments, at the medical profession's urging, had legislated a body of laws severely restricting the medical practices of unorthodox practitioners, and it marked the point when Canadian medical schools started employing full-time teachers and researchers. The choice of 1967 was based on the fact that it was the year that Canada's Medical Act was designed to be implemented, bringing comprehensive national medical and hospital insurance to all citizens. It was symbolic that national health insurance was designed to be phased in during Canada's centennial year - although, because of financing problems, the implementation eventually had to be postponed to 1968.

In Australia, it could be argued that the Labor Party initially attempted to terminate the golden age of medicine with the passing of the National Health Insurance Act in 1948, and again in 1974 with the passing of the Health Insurance Bill. However, while both these Acts provided for a publicly financed health delivery system, the former Act never became operational and the latter created Medibank, which lasted in its original form for only about a year. Consequently, it seems that in Australia, as in the United States, medicine's golden age is still alive, although not necessarily all that healthy.

Recent Perspectives on Medical Technology

The pressures for government assistance in financing health services, which in most countries started in the 1930's during the Great Depression and continued with increasing force up to the early 1970's, were based on an unquestioning belief that more health care meant better health. In Canada, for example, the life expectancy of males at birth increased from 60 in 1931 to 68 in 1961, and it was

[24]

believed (naively in retrospect) that this increase was attributable entirely to more and better care, and not at all to factors like rising affluence and improving hygiene. It was inevitable that, as the access and financing problems concerning health care diminished (at least as far as consumers were concerned) the belief would be subjected to some scrutiny. When this was done it came as a surprise to most people that, at the aggregate level, it was difficult to establish any relationship between the size and quality of a health delivery system and any of the indicators of health standards, like life expectancy. The major exception concerned new-born children, where epidemiologists were able to show that a bigger and better hospital system lowered infant mortality rates. The fact that this relationship was established explains incidentally why infant mortality rates have been commonly used as indicators of the adequacy of health delivery systems.

The disillusionment which people felt on discovering the relative ineffectiveness of modern medicine in resolving man's current batch of problems led to some rather harsh, and probably over-stated, critiques. Probably the best known is that of Ivan Illich. Illich, a philosopher by training, developed the thesis that modern health delivery systems have grown so large that they are currently counter-productive to health. In his words:

> "The medical establishment has become a major threat to health .... A professional and physician-based health care system which has grown beyond tolerable bounds is sickening for three reasons: it must produce clinical damages which must outweigh its potential benefits; it cannot but obscure the political conditions which render society unhealthy; and it tends to expropriate the power of the individual to heal himself and to shape his or her environment" (1975, p.11).

However, there are other critiques of note. Carson, a lawyer, emphasized the notion that health is more influenced by social and environmental factors than by medical care (Carson, 1974). Fox, a sociologist, emphasized the ludicrousness of treating social deviance as disease (Fox, 1977). Finally, Thomas, a physician, described quite succinctly the technical limits of modern medicine:

"The most spectacular technological change has occurred in the management of infectious disease, but its essential features had been solidly established and put to use well before 1950 .... We are left with approximately the same roster of common major diseases which confronted the country in 1950, and, although we have accumulated a formidable body of information about some of them in the intervening time, the accumulation is not yet sufficient to permit either the prevention or the outright cure of any of them" (1977, p.37).

Thomas's observations were directed mainly at the major life-threatening health problems facing mankind - notably heart disease and cancer. It is here where there are large numbers of half-way technologies which can modify the effects of the diseases but which cannot resolve them. Major economic issues arise because invariably the half-way technologies are expensive, often exceeding the financial capacity of individuals and sometimes exceeding the financial capacity of society. But since these technologies are marginal, it is not obvious that they should be supplied in unlimited quantities or at public expense.

While the critiques have centered on medical technology as it relates to the major life-threatening problems, attention has also been given to the minor and largely self-limiting problems which constitute the bulk of a medical practitioner's work. About three quarters of a general practitioner's consultations involve upper respiratory infections, emotional disorders, gastro-intestinal disorders, skin disorders and other minor illnesses (Rogers, 1977). In a surprising number of instances concerning these illnesses, the doctor's therapy is restricted to alleviating pain and discomfort, while letting the illness resolve itself. Recognition of this fact, like recognition of medical technology limitations in dealing with the major health problems, has been conducive to a certain amount of disillusionment about the merits of health care.

Economics and Medical Technology

In view of the technical literature, it is not surprising that, by the early 1970's, most health economists were developing the view that the marginal technical benefit from health services was approaching, if not at, zero. It was a relatively plausible assumption, particularly if technical benefits were thought of in terms of prolonging lives rather than relieving discomfort. The economists' contribution was not to expand on the clinical findings but to explain how the technical over-servicing suggested by people like Illich could be fostered by certain kinds of market arrangements. The explanations depended, in the first instance, on an assumption of ignorant consumers relying on doctors' advice and, in the second, on an assumption of a pricing arrangement which motivated doctors to exploit this ignorance.

The economic analysis, and associated empirical evidence, suggested that the detailed fee-for-service pricing arrangement typically adopted by doctors fosters excess servicing. It encourages practitioners to provide as many services as they can, in order to increase revenues and profits. More significantly, in situations where doctors can induce more demand than they can handle, their optimal behaviour is not to induce less but to eliminate some of the demand by raising prices. Not surprisingly, an unfettered private medical market with fee-for-service pricing tends to be relatively hard on patients because, on the one hand, they are constantly advised to consult the doctor more while, on the other, they are faced with a set of prices which makes this expensive.

The evidence suggesting that fee-for-service induces excess servicing has been accumulating rapidly. For example, it has been known for some time that surgical rates are much higher in Canada and the United States (where fee-for-service is prevalent) than they are in England and Wales (where most doctors are paid either by capitation or by salary - see Bunker, 1970, and Vayda, 1973). The classic Canadian study found that the surgical rate for males was 1.8 times higher in Canada than in England and Wales, and the rate for females was 1.6 times higher (ibid., p.1224). Of course, these are aggregated rates, involving not only elective procedures but also mandatory and/or emergency operations. When the elective procedures are considered separately, the differences tend to be greater. For example, the age standardized number of cholecystectomies per 100,000 British males in 1967 was 27. In Canada the respective number was 135 - five times higher. Similarly the tonsillectomy rate for males in 1967 was 4.6 times higher in Canada than in England and Wales, the hemorrhoidectomy rate was 1.9 times higher, the prostatectomy rate was 2.5 times higher, and so on.

Understandably, the North American medical profession has been reluctant to accept the argument that the variations in surgical patterns are a consequence of payment arrangements. On occasion, they have suggested that the differences reflect variations in the quality of care - an argument that is difficult to either confirm or refute because of the lack of an obvious empirical relationship between the quantity of surgical services and the standard of health. But for what it is worth, the health standards of Britain and North America, as reflected by the traditional indicators (like life expectancy), appear to be remarkably similar. A more subtle argument has been to accept the notion that there is a surplus of surgical services in North America, but to attribute it to a surplus of surgeons rather than to the pricing arrangement.

In the American context, however, the evidence drawn from the health maintenance organizations (HMO's) makes it difficult to accept the above hypothesis. HMO's are organizations designed to supply both health care and health care insurance. The typical HMO is composed of a group of clinics and a hospital. Most HMO's employ salaried doctors although a few obtain medical services from fee-for-service practitioners. The HMO's with salaried doctors are called prepaid group practices (PGP's) while those using fee-for-service arrangements are called foundations for medical care (FMC's). All HMO's provide a specified range of medical and hospital services to members, who enrol by paying a fixed periodic premium.

The most significant economic feature of the PGP's is their comparative inexpensiveness. Many studies, based on different PGP's and employing different empirical methods, have supported the statistical robustness of this conclusion. A study done by Roemer and Dubois established that per capita health expenditures, including both insurance premiums and direct user charges, were 35 percent lower under the Kaiser prepayment plan in California than they were under solo fee-for-service practice in the same area (1969, p.993). A study by Hetherington, involving a comparative analysis of two PGP's with two Blue Cross plans and two commercial insurance plans, identified cost advantages to the former of 46 percent and 29 percent respectively (Hetherington, Hopkins and Roemer, 1975). Finally, a study by Corbin and Krute (1975), which examined matched samples of Medicare beneficiaries (i.e. people over 65 in the United States receiving public benefit payments), found that members of prepayment plans had health care costs 6 to 34 percent lower than those of individuals obtaining care through fee-for-service doctors.

The major determinant of the relatively low PGP costs is their ability to reduce hospitalization. Gaus, for example, compared the hospital experience of Medicaid patients (patients on welfare receiving public benefit payments in the United States) in 10 PGP's with those attending fee-for-service doctors. The former received 340 days of inpatient care annually per 1000 persons while the latter received 888 (Gaus, Cooper and Hirschman, 1976, p.9). Saward established that hospital rates were 69 percent lower in the Kaiser program than in the Blue Cross - Blue Shield program in the same region (Saward, Blank and Lamb, 1972). Finally, Hetherington (1975) found that hospital utilization rates were between 35 and 70 percent lower in PGP's than they were in Blue Cross and commercial insurance plans.

In contrast to the PGP's, the FMC's have cost structures and hospital rates comparable to the general American experience. While many of the studies already cited provide some evidence on this, the study by Gavett and Smith (1968) is particularly instructive since it compares the cost and utilization experiences of one FMC with those of two PGP's in Rochester, New York. Compared to the PGP's, the FMC had costs per enrollee which were 56 percent higher, hospital admissions per member that were 62 percent higher, and a hospital inpatient mix of services which was 12 percent less expensive.

In the face of this evidence, it is difficult to avoid concluding that the way doctors are paid has a major impact on the types and quantities of medical services received by patients. It is also difficult to avoid concluding that fee-for-service, as a volume oriented payment mechanism, is conducive to excess servicing.

Many American health economists and analysts see PGP's as the organizations of the future for constraining rapidly growing health costs and for eliminating excess servicing. While they have much to recommend them, it should not be forgotten that the cost and service benefits that they currently achieve for about 10 percent of Americans the British National Health Service has achieved for a long time for virtually all Britishers. Nevertheless, their achievements are impressive, and awareness of this has played a role in the formulation of health financing policies in Canada and Australia.

CHAPTER 3

THE CANADIAN DEVELOPMENT OF NATIONAL HEALTH INSURANCE

To summarize the discussion and analysis of the last chapter, the period of modern curative medicine started about 1921. By that time medical science was discovering treatments that could alleviate diseases in process, and of course the number of effective treatments increased rapidly during the 1930's and 1940's. Society perceived, and generally over-valued, the worth of these therapies. This generated both benefits and costs for the medical profession. The major benefit was that it allowed medical associations to pursue social policies favoured for both economic and professional reasons. They restricted the ranks of practitioners to those graduating from professionally controlled medical schools and enforced substantial constraints on the business activities of individual doctors. The major cost was that it fostered significant pressure for the public finance of all medical and hospital services, a development which the medical profession opposed.

The evolution of health care finance from the 1920's to the 1980's in large measure reflects the implementation of policies favoured by society and opposed by the profession, although this is not always true and there are many twists and turns along the way.

The 1920's and the First Decade of Modern Curative Medicine

The 1920's in Canada, as in the United States, represented the heyday of the "laissez-faire" philosophy concerning medical practice and policy. Although people accepted the worth of medical services, they did not worry about either the implications of a market philosophy making these services dispensable or the problems arising from professional monopoly control. People did not expect doctors to price medical care out of the reach of patients, although both the philosophy and the control were conducive to this result.

Admittedly, society's faith in the humanitarianism of doctors was to some extent justified, because medical care was supplied in a less commercial manner than it is now. The majority of the doctors were general practitioners who worked in rural and small urban areas and who knew their patients well, socially as well as professionally. The social arrangements meant that prices were rarely dictated by profit considerations alone. Doctors constrained their charges to what was considered fair, which among other things took into account the ability of patients to pay. In many situations doctors found it necessary to accept part of their payment in kind.

Despite the humanitarian behaviour of doctors, some public finance of medical and hospital care did develop during the 1920's, as well as before this. However, it developed not to meet the demands of consumers, as became the case after World War II, but to meet the needs of doctors. Particularly in the western part of Canada which was sparsely populated, it was difficult for a practitioner to make a living through fee-for-service. Many Saskatchewan municipalities very early in the day resolved this problem by paying general practitioners salaries financed through local property taxes. Sarnia, Saskatchewan, which was about to lose its only doctor in 1914, was the first municipality to adopt this procedure. The rural municipal council, without legislative authority, offered him an annual retainer fee of $1,500 (Taylor, 1978, p.70).

The municipal doctor system became general in Saskatchewan in 1916, when a provincial act was passed allowing municipalities to tax finance salaried doctors. In 1919 this act was revised to allow a maximum salary of $4,000 for general practitioner services (ibid.). The system expanded rapidly throughout the province until, by the mid-1930's, it covered approximately one-fifth of Saskatchewan's population.

Similar developments occurred in hospital finance. In 1916 legislative provision was made in Saskatchewan for the combining of towns, villages and rural municipalities into hospital districts for the purpose of financing the erection and maintenance of hospitals. From this arrangement, some municipalities gradually evolved into paying hospital bills for local taxpayers and to collecting the necessary revenue through a land tax. By 1927, at least ten Saskatchewan municipalities were doing this as well as some communities in Manitoba and Alberta (ibid., p.72). By 1934 there were twenty-seven hospital-based prepayment plans operating throughout Canada (Royal Commission on Health Services, 1964, p.386).

The public finance developments of the 1920's must not be blown of proportion, however. For the most part they were confined to Saskatchewan, because of the special economic conditions existing there. In the rest of Canada curative care was considered to be the preserve of the private market, and there was little encroachment on this principle.

The development of public health policies during this period is interesting, considering the prevailing social philosophy. Both federal and provincial public health departments were set up mainly during the 1920's, starting with the creation of a department in New Brunswick in 1917. As noted in the previous chapter, this was after the period when the major public health programs had been implemented. The health departments were really just icing on the cake, their major role being to supervise and co-ordinate programs already in existence. Like most bureaucracies, these departments were interested in expanding their horizons. The problem was where to do this, given that the medical men at the helm of most health departments did not want to intrude on the domain of the profession.

In this context the traditional attitude of the medical profession towards government health policies might be recalled. Since the beginning, doctors had always supported policies involving care for the poor and indigent. It was the medical profession in Britain that, in 1911, brought about capitation to finance care which had originally been charity work. What the profession had always opposed were policies restricting their power to price with respect to patients who could pay.

The attitude of the profession made the direction of expansion of Canadian health departments during the 1920's quite understandable. They became very heavily involved with social welfare programs. These programs concentrated on the poor and disadvantaged, increasing the public finance of health care for these people. In this way, a moral and financial responsibility historically falling on the shoulders of medical practitioners was relieved.

The 1930's and the Great Depression

While ultimately the economic gap between doctors and patients was to widen, during the 1930's it narrowed. The viability of most service industries, including medicine, is very sensitive to the general prosperity of the society. If medical care is a necessity philosophically it is a luxury economically, particularly in relation to severe falls in income. During the 1930's many people did not seek care for conditions that they otherwise would, and, when care was absolutely mandatory, the doctors often found themselves working with little prospect of payment.

The inability of doctors to generate incomes during the 1930's made them more receptive than usual to programs involving public finance. Many writers have commented on the meeting of the Saskatchewan Medical Association in 1933 in which resolutions were put forward providing support for national health insurance (Badgley and Wolfe, 1967, p.12). Also of note were comments of the Canadian Medical Association in 1942 suggesting that capitation or salary might be an appropriate payment mechanism for general practitioners, although not for specialists (Agnew, 1974, p.106).

Partly because of the attitude of the medical profession and partly out of necessity, proposals, policies and programs involving public finance of personal health care became more common during the 1930's. In Saskatchewan, where the effects of the Depression were as severe as anywhere, a number of public programs were either expanded or implemented. In 1931, for example, the Municipal Doctors System was expanded to encompass 52 municipalities (Royal Commission on Health Services, 1964, p.385). In 1932, the Government through its Relief Commission decided on a monthly grant of $75 for doctors in 56 municipalities in Relief Area A and a grant of $50 for doctors in 103 rural municipalities in Relief Area B (Taylor, 1978, p.5). In the same year a Royal Commission on State Health Insurance in British Columbia recommended a national health plan, involving compulsory insurance for all employed persons earning less than $2,400 annually and voluntary insurance for persons earning more than this. While the plan was affirmed in a plebiscite in 1937, it was never introduced into Parliament. In Alberta there were two Commissions of Inquiry favouring health insurance - the first in 1929 and the second in 1933. A Health Insurance Act was passed in 1935, but with the defeat of the Government later in the year it was never implemented. Finally, the Ontario Government in 1935 signed an agreement with the Ontario Medical Association providing for public contributions of $0.35 per person per month, for patients on welfare, to be paid into a medical welfare board administered by the Association. The funds were used to pay doctors for office and home calls.

To many observers the 1930's represent a period of time when the medical profession temporarily modified its views concerning the merits of "socialized medicine". I am more inclined to think that its views during this period were not an aberration but rather an extrapolation of its traditional perspective on policy matters. Doctors had always favoured government finance for patients who could not afford to pay. It was just that under the circumstances this came very close to being a universal plan. Moreover, the profession believed that any scheme worth having would leave practitioners in control of fees. Given the close and symbiotic relationship between medical organizations and health departments, this belief was a natural one.

The 1940's and the Return to Normal Economic Conditions

The return to more prosperous times, particularly after World War II, did not reduce general interest in national health insurance. The Federal Liberal Party proposed a plan at the Federal-Provincial Conference in 1945. The proposal provided federal funds not only for the purpose of maintaining provincially administered plans but also for the purpose of building and modernizing hospitals. It was rejected by the provinces, however, because it was linked with plans to increase federal taxing powers. While it is often assumed that if the proposal had been accepted by provincial governments, its implementation would have been endorsed by the medical profession, it is by no means clear that this was so.

Given the provincial rejection of the national health insurance plan, the federal government in 1948 unilaterally implemented a part of its proposal by introducing a National Health Grant Program. While conditional grants, under which the provinces had to match the federal funds, were made available for a variety of purposes (including most public health and mental health projects), the most important grants involved hospital construction. From 1948 to 1970, when the hospital grants were terminated, federal assistance was provided for over 130,000 beds. Mackenzie King, the Prime Minister at the time that the grant program was implemented, indicated that the augmentation of hospital facilities was the first step in the implementation of a comprehensive health insurance plan for all Canada (Taylor, 1978, p.164).

However, the main impetus for national health insurance during the 1940's shifted from the federal government and the Liberal Party to the Saskatchewan government and the Cooperative Commonwealth Federation Party (CCF). When the CCF Government in Saskatchewan realized that the 1945 federal proposal was doomed to failure, it decided to launch one part of a public health insurance program on its own. In 1946, it passed the Saskatchewan Hospital Act, which brought into operation in 1947 the first universal compulsory hospital insurance program in Canada.

The hospital insurance program was not the only significant policy development which occurred in Saskatchewan in the 1940's. On January 1, 1945, the government arranged with the medical profession the first comprehensive social assistance health services program in Canada. Under the agreement, the government agreed to pay $9.50 annually, per person covered, into a fund from which doctors would then claim for their "charitable" work. While physicians submitted their charges to the fund according to the profession's fee schedule, initially they received only 50 percent of the bill. Then, if there was any money left in the fund at the end of the year, it was sent out to all claiming doctors prorated according to the accounts submitted.

A final important policy innovation for Saskatchewan during the 1940's was the establishment of the Swift Current Health Region as a demonstration project in public medical insurance. On July 1, 1946, all municipal doctor plans in the Swift Current Health Region were integrated in a regional medical care plan, financed by property and personal taxes, and by a subsidy of 10 percent of total cost from the provincial government. The Swift Current Medical Plan was integrated with the Hospital Insurance Plan which started six months later, making Swift Current the first region in Canada to experience comprehensive public health insurance. It is of note that the Swift Current Plan changed the character of the municipal doctor plans, by placing doctors on fee-for-service rather than on fixed annual stipends.

Since the Saskatchewan experience was catalytic to future public policy developments in the rest of Canada, it is difficult if not impossible to avoid stressing the developments that occurred there. However, there are some other provincial policies of interest and significance. It is of particular note that British Columbia followed Saskatchewan very closely by passing a Public Hospital Insurance Act 1948, which led to comprehensive public hospital insurance in 1949. The British Columbia Plan varied from the Saskatchewan Plan in its inclusion of a co-insurance feature (i.e. a hospital user fee). It also varied concerning the method of collecting taxes. Whereas the Saskatchewan Plan employed a compulsory premium, collected by the municipal councils, the British Columbia Plan used a combination of payroll deductions and direct payment. The financing arrangement proved to be unsatisfactory. Not only was it relatively expensive but also it made the relationship between paying and being insured rather tenuous. Because of these problems it was abolished in 1954 in favour of a sales tax.

Other than the Saskatchewan and British Columbia developments, there were only a couple of publicly financed health programs initiated in Canada during the 1940's. One was the Maternity Hospital Care Program set up in Alberta in 1944, which financed standard ward care for all resident maternity cases directly out of provincial general revenues. The other was a system of free diagnostic outpatient services in rural health units set up by Manitoba in 1946.

The 1950's and Public Hospital Insurance

The major impetus for publicly financed health care during the 1940's was society's desire for protection against financial contingencies involving hospital and medical costs. In the absence of public programs, private insurance arrangements developed to meet, at least partly, society's needs. Insurance plans were developed by community organizations, commercial insurers and by the medical profession.

Undoubtedly the most famous community sponsored insurance arrangement was Blue Cross. The first Blue Cross Plan developed in Manitoba in 1939. Subsequent Blue Cross Plans developed in Ontario in 1941, in Quebec in 1942, in the Maritimes and in British Columbia in 1943, and in Alberta in 1948.[12]

In the development of private insurance, there was a noticeable division of the market. Community and commercial insurers concentrated on hospital insurance, while profession-sponsored insurers provided most of the medical insurance. This occurred primarily because the former insurers had no way of controlling physician fees, which was necessary to define a stable relationship between subscriber premiums and insurance coverage. The medical associations could define this relationship by pressing doctors to maintain stable prices in relation to insured patients. The profession sponsored insurers thus had a significant advantage with respect to this type of insurance.

The first profession-sponsored plan developed in Toronto in 1937, and the second in Windsor in 1939. By the end of the 1940's there were nine plans, with a number of them operating on provincial bases. In the early 1950's the profession made an effort to co-ordinate these plans by forming the Trans-Canada Medical Plan (TCMP).

For profit purposes, the medical profession would have preferred to leave medical insurance with the commercial insurers. However, it realized that good private plans were necessary to fight the introduction of socialized medicine. Since good plans implied some control over medical practitioner pricing, the medical organizations were forced to become involved.

The fact that the medical profession became increasingly hostile to public finance of medical care during the 1940's is worthy of comment, since it contrasts with the situation during the 1930's. In the earlier decade, the profession had accepted public finance

---

[12] It is a matter of note that no Blue Cross Plan had developed in Saskatchewan by 1947 and that Blue Cross had managed to insure only 15 percent of the population in British Columbia by 1949. These were the first two provinces with public plans, suggesting that the lack of private options may have at least speeded up the public developments.

because it had realized that it was necessary. Moreover, the profession had implicit faith that it would control all public expenditures since, as one economics committee put it, "what is best for the medical profession must be best for the public" (Canadian Medical Association, 1934, p.4). While the profession undoubtedly continued to believe this during the 1940's, it became increasingly suspicious of society's views - thus the need for the nine professionally sponsored and controlled medical insurance plans. Once these plans were in place, the Canadian Medical Association in 1949 issued a policy statement favouring the use of private voluntary insurance for the majority of Canadians, with premium subsidization by governments only for those individuals who could not afford to buy such insurance (LeClair, 1975, p.13).

The medical profession was not nearly as adamant in its support of private insurance for hospitals as it was for medical services, however. This facilitated the introduction of national hospital insurance during the 1950's considerably.

During this period, there were basically three factors encouraging the federal government to promote public hospital insurance across Canada. First, hospital care was becoming sufficiently expensive, and sufficiently predictable for some groups, that private insurance schemes could not cope with the problem in an adequate way. The people excluded from private insurance were precisely the people who needed financial help most - the poor, the elderly and the chronically ill. [13] Even more important from the perspective of political pressure, most people with insurance found their coverage inadequate. Second, hospitals in the early 1950's were experiencing serious financial difficulties. A major infusion of public money was necessary in one way or another. Support from the Canadian Hospital Association could

---

[13]
    In 1952, 37.6 percent of Canadians had insurance for hospital services, 27.1 percent had insurance for surgical services, and 19.9 percent had insurance for general medical care (Taylor, 1978, p.171).

be counted on for any public policy which increased the revenues of hospitals (LeClair, 1975, p.22). Third, and finally, experience was showing that private insurance was administratively more expensive than public insurance (Taylor, 1978, p.114).

For the above reasons, and because the Saskatchewan and British Columbia hospital plans were popular, the federal government promoted the introduction of national hospital insurance across the country, by passing the Federal Hospital Insurance and Diagnostic Services Act 1957. The HIDS Act offered federal funding to provincial governments conditional on their maintaining hospital insurance plans meeting four basic points (LeClair, 1975). First, all inpatient care in all general hospitals had to be insured. While outpatient services could also be insured under the terms of the Act, this was at the option of the provincial governments. Second, the insurance had to be comprehensive for the services covered, and available on uniform terms and conditions for all citizens. User fees were not precluded, but it was suggested that they be kept low enough not to deter utilization. Third, there had to be portability of insurance, in the sense that individuals travelling or migrating among participating provinces would be assured of continuous coverage. Fourth, and finally, there was an implicit presumption that all plans would be publicly managed.

HIDS offered each provincial government federal funding equal to approximately 50 percent of the operating costs of the hospital insurance plan, excluding depreciation and interest. The amount equalled 25 percent of provincial per capita expenditures plus 25 percent of national per capita expenditures, multiplied by the number of insured persons in the province.

HIDS became operational on July 1, 1958, when Newfoundland, Manitoba, Saskatchewan, Alberta and British Columbia signed agreements. Most of the other provinces joined in the following year - Nova Scotia and Ontario on January 1, New Brunswick on July 1, and Prince Edward Island on October 1. Quebec did not join until January

1, 1961, because of opposition in principle to involvement in cost sharing programs with the federal government.

The 1960's and Medicare

The offer of federal funding through HIDS implied a substantial net increase in revenues for those provinces that were already publicly financing hospitals. This money was catalytic in the further evolution of Canada's health delivery system in that it put Saskatchewan in a financial position where it could reasonably contemplate extending its health insurance system to medical services. Mr T.C. Douglas, the Premier of Saskatchewan, indicated in May 1959 that he was thinking about this, and then in December of the same year he delivered a speech on "Prepaid Medical Care" which left no doubt about the route his government was taking. He proposed a comprehensive medical care program encompassing five basic principles: (1) prepayment, (2) universal coverage, (3) high quality of service, (4) administration by a public body responsible to the legislature, and (5) acceptability both to those providing the service and to those receiving it (Grove, 1969, p.304).

By this time, however, the medical profession had both anticipated, and was in no mood to accept, government intrusion into its markets. In 1955, the Saskatchewan Medical Association had mobilized its monopoly powers by resolving that the profession should act as a whole and that individual doctors and groups should not act on their own without the full approval of the official body (Taylor, 1978, p.259). In 1957, it had indicated dissatisfaction with any government scheme involving a fixed total fund from which an undetermined volume of services had to be financed. This reflected implicitly on the Social Assistance Plan 1945, as well as on the Swift Current program. [14]

---

[14]
The Swift Current Medical Society had accepted the principle of a fixed maximum budget in 1957.

Because the profession had anticipated Premier Douglas's proposal, it responded very quickly and very negatively to it. From the beginning massive public relations activity, and professional refusal to participate in the organization of any public insurance arrangement, were used as methods to scuttle the government's policy. Over the course of the three years during which the legislation and program were formulated, the government became very frustrated with a profession which often refused to even meet, let alone negotiate, and then subsequently threatened not to co-operate because it had not been consulted.

While the profession was opposed to almost all aspects of the government's proposal, its major concern centered on those features which appeared to give to the government power to bargain and act on behalf of patients. It was primarily worried about proposals which appeared to prescribe the financial terms and conditions under which doctors could provide services to insured individuals. It found section 28(a) of the proposed legislation particularly offensive, because it was construed to mean that a government agency could sue a doctor on behalf of a patient (Grove, 1969, p.308).

Because the profession was not offered sufficient control and autonomy, it went on strike when the program was implemented (on July 1, 1962). The strike lasted for 23 days and was resolved when the government, in essence, backed down on its proposal to become a bargaining unit on behalf of patients. A less important concession was the allowance of private insurers which could act as fiscal intermediaries between practising doctors and the government.

While the agreement settling the strike meant that, in theory, doctors retained all the pricing powers that they had had in pre-medicare days, in practice these powers were constrained by two important administrative and institutional policies. First, the government placed a constraint on the use of the bulk billing arrangement. Doctors were allowed to bulk bill the Medical Care Commission only if they accepted the Commission's payments as payments in full. The alternative was to bill patients at any rate desired, and let the patients claim from the Commission. For the doctors, the latter procedure was more expensive administratively, and liable to a certain percentage of bad debts. Second, insurance companies were prohibited from insuring physician charges above the medicare premiums. This made patients more sensitive to private charges, and the process of extra billing less profitable for doctors. At the time, doctors did not object too much to these policies, in large part because the fee schedule adopted by the Commission was extremely generous.

The Saskatchewan Medical Association's fight against medicare from 1959 through 1962 had been supported by the medical profession in all provinces. Indeed, the Canadian Medical Association had donated $35,000 to the SMA's fight against socialism, and had provided a public relations expert so that the campaign might be more effective. In addition, at its Annual Meeting in 1960, it outlined 14 principles which any medical insurance scheme would have to have to be acceptable to the CMA. Since these principles merely formalized earlier views of the organization, they were stated primarily to provide moral support for the profession in Saskatchewan. Finally, the CMA approached the federal government to establish a committee to study the existing and anticipated health needs of Canadians and to study health insurance. Mr Diefenbaker, the Prime Minister, responded by announcing a Royal Commission Study (the Hall Commission) on December 21, 1960. The CMA originally hoped that this would delay, and perhaps scuttle, the Saskatchewan legislation, by forcing the government to wait until the "expert opinion" was in.

When the Saskatchewan Plan was implemented anyway, the opponents of medicare had to organize their opposition differently to prevent public medical insurance from developing general appeal across the country. Renewed efforts were made to develop voluntary plans which not only would be popular with the general public, but which also would be acceptable to the medical profession. Conservative governments in Alberta, Ontario and British Columbia, which were particularly sensitive to the medical profession's problems, all implemented legislation which propped up the profession-sponsored plans in the area where they were most deficient. In Alberta, government subsidies were provided to low income earners to enable them to buy insurance through Medical Services Incorporated (MSI), or through other private insurance arrangements. Rather than using a means test, the subsidy was determined by reference to an individual's past year's income tax statement. Both Ontario and British Columbia established provincial insurance agencies to insure individuals who could not afford private company charges or who were not insurable in the private sector. In Ontario, the program was known as the Ontario Medical Services Insurance Plan (OMSIP) while, in British Columbia, it was known as the British Columbia Medical Plan (BCMP).

The profession plans were dealt a severe blow, however, with the release of the Hall Report in 1964, which favoured the introduction of Saskatchewan type plans across Canada. While the reasons for this decision by the Hall Commission were many, two were particularly significant. First, a comprehensive public plan meant that more people could be insured, and could therefore have access to health care, than was possible under any kind of voluntary private insurance. Second, Saskatchewan's public medical plan, like the public hospital plan preceding it, was proving to be more efficient than the alternative private arrangements.

Given the Hall Report recommendations, and the popularity of the medicare idea with the public, the federal government proceeded with legislation that would make national health insurance a reality across the country. In December, 1966, it passed the Medical Care Act which offered federal financial aid for all provincial medical plans with features comparable to Saskatchewan's. The funding offer for each provincial government equalled 50 percent of the per capita costs over all provincial plans, multiplied by the number of insured

persons. Eventually all provinces accepted the offer - Saskatchewan
and British Columbia on July 1, 1968; Newfoundland, Nova Scotia and
Manitoba, on April 1, 1969; Quebec on November 1, 1970; and Prince
Edward Island on December 1 of the same year.

The Medical Care Act gave careful consideration to user fees,
although its intent was expressed in legally ambiguous terms. The
Act suggested that user fees were permissible:

> "only if they (did) not impede, either by their amount or
> by their method of application, reasonable access to
> necessary medical care, particularly for low income
> groups" (Statistics Canada, 1971, p.332).

Most provinces adopted pricing arrangements comparable to
Saskatchewan's, although the institutional details varied
considerably. Only Quebec adopted more stringent constraints
against physician charges, legislating that if a doctor charged more
than the Commission payments, neither he nor his patients could claim
anything from the Commission.

The Medical Care Act was conducive to all provinces insuring
ambulatory and outpatient hospital services. Although this had been
possible under HIDS, it had been generally not done because it placed
provincial governments in confrontations with the medical
profession. Doctors disliked the HIDS implication of most
pathologists and radiologists becoming salaried hospital employees,
and, of course, in the pre-medicare setting, they saw free outpatient
care as a source of unfair competition. With the introduction of
medicare, both these "problems" disappeared.

It was mentioned above that Quebec, in implementing medicare,
adopted much stricter constraints against private billing than did
other provinces. While Quebec's policy has much to recommend it -
indeed many analysts feel that it is the only viable policy in the
long run - it must not be assumed that it was introduced without
political difficulty. Its implementation was preceeded by a
specialist's strike, starting on August 27, 1970. Fortunately for
the government, the general practitioners decided not to join. This

[46]

was partly because GP's perceived less value in being able to charge in excess of Commission benefits than did specialists, and partly because the GP's were predominantly francophones while there were a significant number of anglophones among the specialists. While the absence of the GP's weakened the strike, it still might have thwarted government legislation if it had not been maintained during the FLQ crisis. However it was, and eventually specialists were ordered back to work, with an agreement less favourable than that which had been offered to them originally. [15]

While the implementation of medicare dominated developments in health care finance during the 1960's there were two other extremely important legislative developments. The first was the Health Resources Fund Act 1965. Under the terms of this Act the federal government assisted in the planning, acquisition, construction, renovation and equipping of health training facilities. In particular, this Act enabled four new medical schools to be built as well as facilitating expansion in the twelve existing schools. Expenditures under this Act were complementary to those under the Medical and Hospital Acts in that they created an increased supply of practitioners to meet the increased demand for health care. The second was the Canada Assistance Plan 1966. It provided for a federal contribution of 50 percent of the provincial public cost of assistance to persons in need. A number of expenditures under this plan, like those on prescription drugs and nursing home care, was in the domain of health finance.

15

The original Quebec proposal was much like the legislation that finally emerged - that is to say it was proposed that, if a doctor billed a patient for more than the medicare fees, then not only the doctor but also the patient could claim nothing from the Commission. However, when doctors reacted negatively to the proposal, the government, on June 25, 1970 modified it. Under the modified proposal, 3 percent of physicians in any specialty and in any administrative region could opt out, with patients of the opted out physicians receiving public benefits equal to 75 percent of the general level. When the profession went on strike the government basically reverted to its original policy.

The 1970's and National Health Insurance

By the early 1970's, Canada had pretty much established a national health insurance system, and had done this through the mechanism of federal conditional grants. Under the circumstances, it might have seemed reasonable to leave the funding arrangement alone, at least for a while, to see how it would fare. However, this was not to be. There were at least three factors conducive to change. First, there was the changing perception of the effectiveness of medical technology. As long as health care financing was a private matter, governments could ignore the increasing number of critiques on medicine. But when health financing became public, they could not because it had implications for how efficiently public dollars were being perceived to be spent. The influence of changing perceptions about medical technology was reflected in the 1974 working paper of the Federal Minister of Health, entitled A New Perspective on the Health of Canadians, A Working Document (Lalonde, 1974). This paper suggested that, over the long haul, more public dollars should be spent on preventative health and fewer on curative care. The second factor conducive to changing the funding arrangement for health was the political difficulty which the federal government had in maintaining any kind of cost sharing arrangement with Quebec. The third was the perceived high cost and open-ended nature of conditional funding. Both these latter forces grew rapidly in importance during the 1970's, exacerbated by the rapidly rising energy prices starting in 1973 and by the major slow-down in economic growth exhibited later during the decade.

Federal problems in co-ordinating programs with Quebec were, of course, in evidence before the 1970's. Of particular note in this regard was the Established Programs (Interim Arrangements) Act 1965, which was legislated by the federal government specifically to meet the demands of Quebec. It allowed any province to opt out of the hospital insurance program (HIDS), in the sense of accepting 14 percentage points of the personal income tax, equalized to the yield of the same number of points in the two highest income provinces, in lieu of the conditional grant. [16] While the opting out arrangement was offered to all provinces, it was attractive only to Quebec. It led to a situation where Ottawa could maintain that the tax transfer was an abatement which could be withdrawn, while Quebec could argue that the tax revenue was a constitutional right. The other provinces did not opt out because of a fear that it would lead to a reduction in federal payments.

The 1965 Act was significant in two ways. First, it led to a situation where, from January 1, 1965 to March 31, 1977, federal payments to Quebec were established differently from those of other provinces. [17] Particularly the western provinces resented this fact increasingly as time went on. Second, it provided a precedent for considering opting out to be a substitute for a conditional grant - thus playing an important role in the formulation of Established Program Financing in 1977.

The 1965 Act also created the notion of an established program, although the full implications of this were not to be fully appreciated until much later. An established program meant any program in which a federal presence was no longer considered necessary to ensure its continuance. In the case of hospital care it was believed that any substantial cut-back in services or coverage would bring forth such a storm of public protest that no provincial government would attempt it.

The more pressing reason for phasing out cost sharing grants, however, was not Quebec's opposition to them but a fear that they were leading to inadequate budgetary control. Prior to 1977, there was

---

16

While the Established Programs (Interim Arrangements) Act was applicable to a number of conditional grant programs, it is only the hospital grant which is of interest here.

17

The federal government always maintained, however, that its different way of funding Quebec did not affect the amount of the intergovernmental fiscal transfer. Whether this was true or not, it is significant that a number of politicians and policymakers, particularly in Western Canada, were inclined to be sceptical.

much talk about provinces spending 50 cent dollars, and about health care costs soaring out of control. At a 1976 Conference of federal and provincial first ministers, Prime Minister Trudeau enumerated seven major difficulties with cost sharing, of which three reflected his concern about the open-ended nature of the federal commitment (Trudeau, 1977, p.248). The federal government had, by the time of this speech, already taken some preliminary steps to deal with the perceived problem. Maximum allowable growth rates in federal contributions for medicare, of 13.0 percent for 1976-77 and 10.5 percent for 1977-78, had been specified. Also, notice had been served that the hospital agreements with the provinces would be terminated at the earliest possible date - which was 1980.

Thus, by 1976, it was clear that the federal government was planning to modify its funding commitment for health. Its plans ultimately resulted in the Federal Provincial Fiscal Arrangements and Established Programs Financing Act 1977. While the details of this Act are extremely complex, its general impact is easily enough described. First, it grouped three of Canada's major conditional grant programs, involving hospital insurance, medical insurance, and post-secondary education finance, into one. Second, the cost sharing features in place prior to 1977 were replaced by formula funding. Specifically, the federal payment for all three programs was defined in per capita terms, with the annual rate of increase defined by an escalator based on gross national product. Third, the federal contribution was designed to be provided about half in the form of cash payments and the other half in the form of tax transfers (it was this feature which accounted for most of the Act's legislative complexity).

The objectives for and impact on health of EPF turned out to be controversial. The basic issue was whether EPF represented unconditional or conditional funding. The fact that the programs were defined as "established", the fact that health and education funding were grouped together, the fact that the amount of provincial financial support was determined on a per capita basis, and the fact that tax transfers were involved, all tended to suggest that EPF moneys were unconditional. On the other hand, the fact that the funds were ear-marked, and the fact that the four conditions concerning health standards were retained in the 1977 Act, implied the opposite. The federal government's propensity to vacillate on the matter, depending on the political situation, exacerbated, rather than diminished, the controversy.

The disputes over the intent of EPF had their counterparts in the discussion on effects. Here, the issue was not what happened after EPF, but whether EPF was a determining factor. Specifically, did EPF contribute to most provincial governments tightening their budgets for each of their established programs, and did it contribute to their becoming more lax about the increasing prevalence of private billing by doctors? My inclination is to respond affirmatively to both these questions, because the shift from cost sharing to formula funding under EPF removed all financial incentive for provincial governments to resist these trends. On the other hand, many analysts are inclined to dismiss the importance of the financial inducement associated with cost sharing. They suggest that the late 1970's trends would have developed with or without EPF, because of the recessionary forces and the increasingly conservative ethic which were under way. In earlier work, I summarized the controversy in the following manner:

> "The question of whether EPF has contributed to the stringent budgets for the established programs unfortunately remains a controversial issue. We know that EPF gives the provinces added flexibility for constraining the growth rates of funds to these programs. We also know that EPF has led to a pattern of federal-provincial funding which could not possibly exist under cost sharing. What we don't know is, if the pre-1977 financing format had been maintained, whether the Federal Government would have contributed less to the established programs, or whether the provincial governments would have spent more. Probably the best guess is that some combination of the two would have occurred" (Brown, 1982, p.109).

The summary remains a fair description of the situation.

The 1980's: Problems and Prospects

In the last section, reference was made to the fact that private billing by doctors increased in prevalence and in amount after 1977. It must not be deduced from this that private billing has already seriously compromised the objectives and effectiveness of Canada's national health insurance system. It has not. The amount of private billing, compared to amounts in countries like Australia and the United States, remains remarkably low. The data in Table 3-1 indicate that in no Canadian province is the amount of private billing as high as 5 percent of cost, and in some provinces, like Quebec and British Columbia, it is virtually non-existent. What is at issue is that, as long as provincial governments are unwilling to formally constrain physician pricing powers, medicare retains the potential for shifting from an insurance plan for patients to a subsidization plan for medical practitioners.

The prospects for provincial governments dealing more aggressively with medical associations are unfortunately not good, at least for the foreseeable future. The recessionary forces and the diminished growth rate of GNP, which have continued since the mid-1970's, are having noticeable effects on the standards of living of most individuals. Many middle and high income people have responded to the problem by becoming more conservative. They are currently favouring lower tax rates, and correspondingly lower expenditures on public programs which are perceived to transfer income from themselves to others. While social welfare programs are most affected by this change in attitude, expenditures on health insurance and post-secondary education are also affected. It is difficult for a provincial government to get electoral support for aggressive dealings with the medical profession in such an environment, even if it is interested in maintaining the viability of public health insurance - and, unfortunately, there are a number of instances where the provincial governments are not.

Table 3-1: Number of Doctors Private Billing, and the Value of Private Billing, by Province and Territory, March 31, 1981

Province	Doctors		Private Billing	
	Number	Percent of Doctors in Province	Amount $	Percent of Medicare Payments
Newfoundland	2	0.5	80,000	0.3
Prince Edward Island	8	5.8	200,000	2.2
Nova Scotia	663	52.8	2,800,000	3.5
New Brunswick	83	13.7	100,000	0.2
Quebec	49	0.5	n.a.	n.a.
Ontario	1,997	15.5	40,000,000	3.5
Manitoba	96	5.9	1,200,000	1.1
Saskatchewan	350	30.7	2,100,000	2.3
Alberta	994	44.1	8,200,000	4.8
British Columbia	1	0.0	n.a.	n.a.
Yukon	0	0.0	0	0.0
North West Territories	0	0.0	0	0.0

Source: National Council of Welfare, 1982, Appendix B, p.68

As far as the federal government is concerned, its role in the finance and operation of the national health insurance system remains ambiguous. Its 1982 legislation revising and extending inter-governmental fiscal arrangements for another five years, basically left the format of EPF funding unchanged, but reduced the amount of effective federal support by removing a revenue guarantee which had been in the arrangement since 1972. Reduced federal support might be construed to imply more private funding, other things being equal. On the other hand, the federal government has stated that it wants new legislation in place by March 31, 1983, where the national standards for health care will be clarified and an effective mechanism for their maintenance will be developed. What this implies is difficult to say, both because it is not clear what the federal government has in mind, and because it is not clear what the provincial governments can be persuaded to agree to.

CHAPTER 4

THE EVOLUTION OF AUSTRALIAN HEALTH INSURANCE POLICIES

As mentioned in Chapter 2, by 1921 two basic models for the finance of health care had evolved - the British model and the American model. The Australian financing arrangement in place at this time had incorporated a number of features of the British system not in evidence in Canada. It had a system of public and private hospitals, it had a tradition of most private practice doctors donating a portion of their time to the public hospitals, and it had a network of friendly societies which obtained medical services by paying doctors capitation fees.

With respect to hospital practices, Australia had developed a system somewhere in between British and North American traditions. As mentioned in Chapter 2, Britain during the nineteenth century had three kinds of hospitals - municipal, voluntary and private - while the United States and Canada had basically only one. Australia was in between with its dual system of public and private institutions. Australia's system was like Britain's in that it differentiated between charity and other patients, but unlike it in that it did not distinguish between the undeserving and the deserving poor. Australia's public hospitals were originally set up to provide free hospital and medical services to all patients in the "labouring classes", and in this sense were a composite of the British municipal and voluntary institutions. [18] In Australia as elsewhere, of course, the private hospitals were developed primarily to facilitate

---

[18]
  The discussion in the text is not meant to imply that Australians did not conceive of a difference between deserving and undeserving poor. Indeed they did and, formally speaking, Australia's public hospitals were intended only for the deserving poor (Roe, 1976a, p.13). However, in practice the large public hospitals accepted virtually all who applied, with little or no question as to why they could not pay, or indeed as to whether they could not pay (Dickey, 1976, p.66).

doctors' provision of surgical services to affluent patients on a fee-for-service basis. [19]

In Britain, it will be recalled, the municipal hospitals were basically taxed financed institutions which employed doctors on a salaried basis while the voluntary hospitals were donation financed institutions which provided medical services via the charitable acts of private practice doctors. The composite nature of Australia's public hospitals were evidenced both by the ways that they received their operating funds and by the ways in which they obtained physician labour. Funds came partly from private donations and partly from governments, although the latter grew in relative importance over time, until by the early 1900's, it was the dominant source of funding. By 1911 in New South Wales, for example, the public hospitals received £153,000 from government sources, £120,000 from subscriptions, £39,000 from patients, and £16,000 from other sources (Dickey, 1976, p.67). Private practice doctors contributed to the charitable functions of public hospitals by functioning as honorary staff, although their services were supplemented by those of salaried physicians.

The medical staffing procedures of Australian public hospitals evolved during the latter part of the nineteenth century, as medical considerations increasingly dominated social considerations as reasons for hospitalizing patients. Non-charity patients were introduced into the public hospitals in increasing numbers, typically as private patients of the honorary staff. The private patients, in contrast to the public patients, were expected to pay both hospital and medical bills - where the bills were submitted separately by the hospitals and doctors concerned. The honorary staff highly valued the right of admitting private patients, and over time came to see this right as their return for providing free care to public patients.

---

[19]
For general discussions on the history of Australian public and private hospitals see Dewdney (1972) and Commonwealth Department of Health (1978) particularly pp.108-124.

As the practice of differentiating between public and private patients evolved, the honorary staff developed mixed feelings about the role of salaried physicians. They appreciated them to the extent that they cared for public patients, and thus reduced the amount of medical care that had to be provided on a free basis. On the other hand, they were suspicious that salaried doctors might be used for patients who could afford to pay (ibid., p.66; and Bell, 1976, p.287).

In most public hospitals a tradition developed in which some wards were defined as public, and were reserved for low-income patients who were identified through a means test. The remaining private wards were provided to patients who could afford to pay, both for their accommodation and for their medical treatment. The mix of public and private beds in turn largely defined the complement of salaried physicians that a hospital found optimal.

The above developments meant that salaried hospital doctors were more in evidence in Australia than in Canada by the early 1920's, although they played a smaller role in Australia than was the case in Britain.

A final way in which Australian pre-1921 practices reflected British traditions was the development of the friendly societies. These societies were basically non-profit insurers of medical care. They provided a specified range of services to subscribers for fixed periodic premiums, and they obtained these services from private practitioners by means of contracts involving capitation payments.[20]

The friendly societies first appeared in Australia in the 1830's, and grew rapidly in importance until by 1910 they accounted for approximately one-third of the population. They diminished in

---

[20]

For a detailed discussion on the friendly societies in Australia, as well as their relationship to the medical profession, see Pensabene (1980, pp.147-158).

importance after that point, for all practical purposes disappearing from the scene in the late 1940's.

It is not coincidental that the friendly societies gradually disappeared with the ushering in of medicine's golden age. In the nineteenth century, the medical profession had supported the friendly societies in their inducement of thrift and self-reliance among the working classes, which reduced the need for charity. But the profession also felt that these organizations were not the appropriate means through which high income earners should receive their medical care. All through the nineteenth century, doctors and their organizations continually pressed for legislation and policies which would constrain the operations of friendly societies to low income people, and which would require these societies to offer doctors capitation payments above competitive levels. But doctors were not in sufficiently high repute, nor were they in sufficient control of their numbers, to achieve these objectives. Competition was the rule of the day, and it worked to the benefit of patient-consumers. But, unfortunately, as the respect for medical technology increased, this changed. In 1918, for example, Victoria legislated an income limit concerning eligibility for membership in a friendly society - which, among other things, formalized the notion of two standards of care (Pensabene, 1980, p.155). However, the important factor in the friendly societies' gradual demise was not legislation of this sort, but legislation which gave the profession effective control over its numbers. As medical manpower supply was curtailed, fee-for-service practice became more lucrative and it became increasingly difficult for the societies to find doctors who would accept capitation contracts. As early as 1914 in New South Wales, the strength of the Medical Association was such that it could get all doctors to withdraw from society practices, until the latter organizations yielded to its monetary demands (Dickey, 1976, p.68). As the medical associations in Australia strengthened the friendly societies weakened, until the capitation contracts disappeared from the scene in 1947.

Although friendly societies with capitation contracts are no more in Australia, they continue to have a bearing on public policy. The form of health funding which they developed is simultaneously favoured by many analysts, who see it as an optimal way of constraining the growth rate of medical costs, and feared by doctors, who see it as a procedure for diminishing their control over medical markets. In this regard, the American experience with health maintenance organizations looms large, for the HMO in many respects appears as a modern day equivalent of the traditional friendly society.

The above evidence must not be taken to imply that Australia was either ahead of or behind Canada and the United States in terms of its health care policies prior to 1921 - not that it would have mattered much if it had been, given the inadequacy of medical technology. The phenomena of salaried doctors, free hospital services for the poor, and friendly societies, in Australia and Britain but not in Canada and the United States, reflected not so much a variation in the enlightenment of social policy as a variation in the state of socio-economic conditions. Because of the enclosure movement, Britain had a surplus of unemployed and poor people which, at least initially, flowed through to Australia through Britain's convict policy. Except perhaps in the American south (where blacks were employed as slaves on the plantations) there was no North American counterpart to the Australian labour situation. Most workers in Canada and the United States opted for self-employment, and the few who did not found wage prospects extremely good by international standards. Free, or subsidized, health care was simply not as necessary in North America as it was in Australia and England.

The existence in Australia and Britain of relative labour availability, and relative poverty among the working classes, fostered not only micro-developments like salaried doctors and friendly societies but also macro-developments like labour movements as political parties. [21] Indeed, it is of note that the Australian Labor Party was probably the dominant political force in

Australia from 1901 to 1914, both at state and at federal levels. [22]
Whether Canada and the United States, with their absences of labour
parties, lagged behind Australia concerning social policies during
this period is debatable - although I personally think not. But there
is little doubt that the formation of labour parties affected the way
social programs were perceived. The development of both the
Australian and British Labor Parties, reflecting views about the
inevitability of class conflict, fostered a perception that social
programs were intended for the working man, and were inherently in
conflict with the interests of all other groups. Remnants of this
view remain to this day (Truman, 1969, p.255). In Australia, the view
has been conducive to associating the rate of social progress with
the electoral success of the Labor Party, a perception which has no
close counterpart in Canada.

"Laissez-Faire" Medicine: 1921-1941

In Australia, as in Canada, Britain and the United States, the
1920's and 1930's were years when the medical profession was given
maximum power to control health care markets in its own interest. As
a consequence there was very little social policy, in the sense of
governments attempting to regulate or supplant markets in situations
where their functioning implied unacceptable hardships for
patient-consumers. It was not until the 1940's that persistent
efforts of this sort arose.

21

For an historical discussion indicating that, by the latter part of
the nineteenth century, Australia already had become a highly
urbanized country, had a large employed working class, and was well
along in the process of developing a Labor Party, see Clark (1980)
particularly chapter 9, but also chapters 5 and 10. This evidence
is consistent with the view about Australian socio-economic
development that I am offering in the text, but obviously is not
synonymous with it. Responsibility for the view must remain my
own. It is a responsibility of some weight, given that the view is
not a common one. The more common view is that Australian
turn-of-the century labour conditions were more comparable to
North America's than to Britain's.

22

See Roe (1976a) for a discussion which emphasizes the role of the
Australian Labor Party in the development of social programs over
the 1901-1914 period.

It is possible, however, to glean from the pre-1941 years signs of a beginning of a public policy approach to health care. In this context, one can go back as far as 1905-1914 when Labor governments in both New South Wales and Queensland pressed for the introduction of free hospital care (Dickey, 1976; and Bell, 1976). As their efforts were not immediately successful, the major effect was to familiarize people with the notion of a public policy option in the provision of hospital services.

While the initial policy moves towards free hospital care were more auspicious in New South Wales than in Queensland, they were ultimately to be more successful in the latter state. [23] The beginning of the evolution towards free hospital care in Queensland occurred in 1905, when a Labor/Country Party coalition government was elected, and a number of the Labor members of parliament began to press for a free hospital system. Although Labor remained in power (eventually independently of the support of the Country Party), not much happened until 1916, when a Hospitals Bill was passed. This Bill specified that one-third of public hospitals' funds should come from the government, one-third from the local authorities, and one-third from voluntary subscriptions (which, if not received, were to be made up by the government and the local authorities). After substantial government support of public hospitals had been arranged, it was reasonable to press also for government administrative control. The 1923 Hospital Act, which separated Queensland into hospital districts, promoted this result. Each district was managed by a hospital board, which controlled all the public hospitals within its boundaries, and which nominated local committees to manage individual hospitals. The board itself was composed of three government representatives, three local authority representatives, and three members elected by direct vote, and was answerable to the Minister of Health and Home Affairs in Brisbane. Financial matters

---

23

The paragraph in the text provides only a thumbnail sketch of the evolution of Queensland's public hospital system. Readers interested in additional detail should see Bell's article (1976).

occupied most of the boards' attention. In 1936, the government introduced another Hospital Bill, which strengthened government control over the boards, by specifying that their chairmen would subsequently be appointed by the Governor-in-Council rather than by election by board members. The Bill also empowered the boards to change hospital medical staffing procedures from the honorary system to one involving full-time salaried appointments, a power which was to have a substantial impact on hospital staffing procedures. By 1940-41, salaried doctors constituted 60 percent of Queensland's public hospital medical staff - a marked contrast to the 20 percent in New South Wales, 23 percent in both Victoria and South Australia, 25 percent in Western Australia, and 37 percent in Tasmania (Commonwealth Bureau of Census and Statistics, 1943, p.196). The extensive use of salaried hospital doctors in Queensland facilitated its introduction of a free hospital system in 1944, available to any state resident prepared to stay in a public bed.

As far as the Commonwealth government during the 1921-1941 period was concerned, it was dominated by conservative parties which had a strong belief in the value of the unfettered market, at least in relation to social programs. Initially, insofar as these parties showed any interest in social policies, they favoured private programs, funded through voluntary insurance principles. In the area of medical care there was considerable irony in this, in that the medical profession was doing everything it could to reduce the viability of the friendly societies, and the Commonwealth government did nothing to offset the profession's anti-market activities.

As the period progressed, and the lack of viability of the "laissez-faire" approach became increasingly apparent, there were some isolated efforts at government action involving national insurance, based on the notion of compulsory enrolment and premium payments by most individuals (Dewdney, 1972, pp.29-31). This course of action was reflected in the National Insurance Bill 1928, which specified insurance cover for sickness, invalidity and maternity, among other things. It was also reflected in the National Health and

<u>Pensions Bill</u> 1938, which included free medical attendance and treatment for insured persons. However, the first Bill was never passed and the second was never implemented, primarily because the more conservative groups in society recognized the programs for what they were - basically tax-financed social programs which were being presented as insurance arrangements for the purpose of political viability. [24] However, the opposition of the medical profession to those parts of the Bills relating to health care also played a role. Finally, insofar as the 1938 Bill was concerned, there were major funding problems because of the constraining effect which the Great Depression had had on national income.

A Beginning to National Health Insurance: 1941-1949

In historical context, the 1941-1949 period seemed a propitious time for the introduction of national health insurance in Australia. Part of the reason for this was the existence of the Labor government, which was committed to the establishment of a "free" national health service. But having a Labor government was clearly not enough. Australia had had Labor governments before, and they had made little headway with the public finance of health care. What made the period seem propitious was the combined experiences from the Great Depression and World War II. The experience of the Depression exposed the weaknesses in conservative arguments that the private market economy was basically a self-rectifying mechanism, and that voluntary insurance could meet all financial contingencies arising from economic fluctuations. In 1936, the economist J.M. Keynes provided a theoretical basis for public expenditure intervention

---

[24]
An advocate of national health insurance during the 1930's noted that "real insurance requires that individuals who are to be protected from loss should contribute mathematically calculated premiums to a reserve from which individual losses are to be made good", and went on to argue correctly that few social problems are insurable in this sense (Wood, 1976, p.205).

Over the years, publicly financed health programs in both Australia and Canada have generally been euphemistically labelled national insurance programs rather than national health service programs, to get around the stigma of socialism and the welfare state.

into a market economy, and the subsequent public expenditure programs generated out of necessity by World War II seemed to validate his theoretical approach (Keynes, 1936).

While the Keynesian interventionist approach was directed mainly at employment issues (with consequent implications for the role of unemployment insurance), it was inevitable that the arguments and rationales should spill over to other social programs. Thus the Labor government during the 1940's pressed for a tax financed "free" health care service, in the belief that the rationale of such an approach would not have to be defended against discredited conservative criticisms.

World War II had two other effects conducive to the introduction of national health insurance. First, the objective of winning the war necessitated a substantial degree of economic planning and a corresponding mobilization of a civil service with a wide spectrum of talents and capacities. The new planning bureaucracy, which found it necessary to supplant the market for war-time purposes, subsequently found it easy to consider the same technique for the wide array of social programs favoured by the Labor Party (Roe, 1976b, p.221). Second, the war necessitated large increases in tax rates and revenues, which it was easy to subsequently allocate to social services. In this regard, the 1943 decision of the Australian government to establish a National Welfare Fund is of note. In the early stages, the Fund received the lesser of one-quarter of the total personal income tax collections or £30 million annually for the purpose of financing a variety of welfare schemes (Dewdney, 1972, p.34). The accumulation of funds in this way meant that the financial implications of the Australian government's health legislation later in the decade was not a pressing problem - a situation which reformist governments rarely find themselves in.

When the Labor government eventually attempted to introduce a national health service, it pressed forward more or less simultaneously on three separate fronts. In 1944, it passed the

Pharmaceutical Benefits Act, which provided for the free provision of medicines and prostheses listed on a government formulary, if prescribed by a doctor. In 1945, it entered into agreements with the states whereby it paid them six shillings a day per patient occupying beds in both public and private hospitals, provided that they waived all charges to those accommodated in public beds in public hospitals. Finally, during 1945-48 it pressed for an agreement with the Medical Association involving the provision of tax financed medical services, but was never able to achieve one.

In fact, the Labor government's policies were frustrated in all areas where they required the co-operation of the medical profession. This affected not only the goal of free medical services but also the goal of free drugs and appliances. When the Pharmaceutical Benefits Act was passed in 1944, the profession refused to comply with it, suggesting that a restricted formulary interfered with a doctor's freedom to prescribe what he thought was best for his patients, and that the use of official forms interfered with a doctor's personal freedoms. As a consequence of the efforts of the Medical Society of Victoria, the Act in 1945 was brought before the High Court of Australia, which declared it invalid on the grounds that it controlled the conduct of doctors and pharmacists, as well as that of persons dealing with them. According to Australia's constitution this was a power available only to the state governments, and not to the Commonwealth government.

The High Court decision forced the Labor government to seek a constitutional change in 1946, through a social services referendum. The referendum was successful and gave the Commonwealth parliament the power to make laws with respect to:

> "the provision of maternity allowances, widows' pensions, child endowment, unemployment, pharmaceutical, sickness and hospital benefits, medical and dental services (but not so as to authorize any form of civil conscription), benefits to students and family allowances" (ibid., p.35).

The success of the referendum encouraged the government to try again to implement a medicaments program, through the Pharmaceutical Benefits Act 1947. However, 90 percent of the doctors still refused to co-operate and eventually (in 1949) had the Act declared invalid, on the grounds that requiring practitioners to write out prescriptions on a prescribed form constituted a form of civil conscription.

Perhaps more than any other event during the 1940's, the 1949 Court decision was a testimony to the political sophistication of the Australian medical profession. When the 1946 referendum had first been proposed, the words in brackets about civil conscription had not been included. They were suggested by the President of the British Medical Association in Australia to Mr Menzies, the Leader of the Opposition, who then proposed them to Parliament. They were accepted by the government without much debate, in large measure because the Labor Party was relieved that the referendum was going forward with a minimum of fuss.

Despite all the difficulties which the government faced in dealing with the profession, it made one last effort at introducing a comprehensive publicly financed health delivery system in 1948, by having a National Health Service Act passed. Among other things, this Act allowed the Commonwealth to take over, establish, maintain and manage hospitals; and to meet a proportion of doctors' charges provided that prescribed fees were levied. The enabling powers of the Act were never utilized, in part because of the Labor government's defeat at the polls in December, 1949.

Subsidized Private Insurance: 1949-1972

The incoming Liberal/Country Party Government, elected in 1949, recognized the general popularity of the Labor Party's proposals in the area of health care. It thus set out to lower the costs of health services in ways that would not offend the medical profession, private insurers, and other powerful political groups. In the main, this meant heavily subsidizing the existing private insurance arrangements, but it also implied public funding for the health services of disadvantaged groups which private insurance either would not or could not reach. The approach was acceptable to conservative groups because it was perceived to supplement the operations of private markets rather than to supplant them.

In the area of prescribed drugs, the new approach meant very little change from Labor policy. In September, 1950, a general pharmaceutical benefits scheme was implemented, which differed from the 1944 and 1947 schemes primarily in that it comprised a smaller list of eligible drugs, and in that it allowed doctors to write prescriptions on private as well as government forms (Kewley, 1965, pp.346-347). The new scheme was supported by the medical profession, suggesting that its earlier opposition had not been based on a perception of intrinsic faults in a system of free drugs but on a perception that, under Labor, such a system represented the first step in phasing in a nationalized medical service.

In 1952, the Liberal/Country Party Government effectively modified the hospital agreements in existence with the states. At that point, it was necessary for the Commonwealth to increase its state hospital grants from eight shillings per patient per day (the level which had existed since 1948) to 12, if it expected to maintain its share of hospital costs. Rather than doing this, it allocated the funds to subsidizing registered voluntary non-profit insurers. Patients who were enrolled with such insurers thus found themselves getting, in addition to the insurer benefit of six shillings for each day spent in a hospital, an additional four shillings in the form of a Commonwealth benefit (paid through the insurer). [25] The states, for their part, were no longer committed to offering free public bed accommodation, and all states except Queensland reinstituted charges.

---

[25]
    After this point, the Commonwealth grant to the state was known as the "ordinary benefit", while the grant to the patient through the insurer was known as the "additional hospital benefit" (Dewdney, 1972, p.41).

In 1953, the government implemented a voluntary medical benefits scheme, which subsidized private medical insurance in much the same way that the agreements of the previous year had subsidized private hospital insurance. After July 1, 1953, privately insured patients, upon presenting doctors' bills, received from their funds both private and Commonwealth benefits. Rather oddly, the benefits scheme had no mechanism for ensuring that the amount of medical insurance coverage was adequate, but did have a mechanism for ensuring that the two benefits together could not exceed 90 percent of physician charges (Deeble, 1970, pp.55-56).

From the start, the government was aware of the fact that its voluntary insurance approach would not be adequate for most elderly people. Because of this, in February, 1951, it set up a special Pensioner Medical Service, designed to provide free general practitioner type services to pensioners and their dependants. Doctors who agreed to participate in the program were paid directly by the Commonwealth government, on a concessional fee-for-service basis. When the hospital agreements were modified in 1952, the government then made special arrangements so that people under the Pensioner Medical Service would continue to get free public bed care. Grants to the states, insofar as they related to pensioners and their dependants, were increased to twelve shillings per day while, it will be recalled, grants for other hospital patients were left at eight shillings.

All of the major components of the Liberal/Country Party government's health program - the pharmaceutical benefits scheme, the modified hospital agreements, the voluntary medical benefits scheme, and the Pensioner Medical Service - were implemented initially under the powers bestowed on the government by the National Health Services Act 1948. It was not until November, 1953, that the various schemes were encompassed in a new piece of legislation passed by Parliament. This was the National Health Act 1953, which became the basis for all Australian health care policy to 1975, although the legislation was amended from time to time.

None of the components of the government's health program proved free of economic and political difficulties. Consider first the pharmaceutical benefits program. Its major problem was that it expanded rapidly in cost, always pressing the government's willingness and/or capacity to pay. Costs increased from £9.2 million in 1953-54 to £21.0 million in 1958-59, and this occurred in spite of a variety of moves by the government to constrain costs (Kewley, 1965, p.349). A thumbnail sketch of government actions with respect to its pharmaceutical scheme is as follows. In 1952, the second year of operation of the scheme, the list of eligible drugs was expanded substantially, as far as pensioners and their dependants were concerned. The creation of two classes of benefits- General Pharmaceutical Benefits and Pensioner Pharmaceutical Benefits - was, of course, a policy which increased costs. However, in 1955, eligibility for coverage in the Pensioner Medical Service was substantially restricted - an action which constrained costs. Finally, in 1959, the government expanded the list of eligible drugs to almost all of the medicaments in the British Pharmacopoeia. At the same time, however, it levied a user charge of five shillings per prescription for all non-pensioner users.This charge was subsequently increased - to $1.00 in 1971 and to $2.00 in 1976.

It was mentioned in the preceding paragraph that, in 1955, eligibility for the Pensioner Medical Service was significantly restricted. When the program was originally implemented, an eligible pensioner included any person in receipt of an old age, invalid, widow's or service pension, or a tuberculosis allowance. Eligible dependants included the spouse and all children under 16 living at home. As time went on, the Australian Medical Association (which, by this time, had succeeded the British Medical Association in Australia) became progressively less happy about this, because it felt that the Service was not sufficiently restricted to people in poor circumstances. Partly in response to AMA pressure, the government in 1955 imposed a special means test - effectively limiting eligibility for single individuals to those making less than £2 per week, and for married couples to those making less than £4 (ibid., p.369).

While the Pensioner Medical Service partially alleviated the inherent weakness in the subsidized voluntary health insurance approach as it affected the poor, it did nothing for people precluded from buying private insurance by virtue of pre-existing ailments. To deal with this problem, both for hospital and medical insurance, the government in 1958 passed amending legislation to the National Health Act. Basically, the amendment allowed the private funds to place people with chronic or pre-existing ailments in special accounts. If, at the end of the financial year, activities in these special accounts led to deficits, the extra cost was financed by Commonwealth reimbursements.

Despite the efforts of the government to make subsidized voluntary insurance an effective health financing arrangement for all Australians, a continuing criticism of the system was that it was not successful. As of the mid-1960's, membership in the private funds represented about 73 percent of the population, and people eligible for care under the Pensioner Medical Service accounted for another 8 percent (ibid., p.366). This left 19 percent of Australia's population without much benefit from the government's health policies, of which a large proportion came from the poor and disadvantaged sections of the community.

A final glaring weakness of the subsidized voluntary health insurance approach was that it prevented the government from ever achieving high levels of protection from medical care costs. The combining fund and Commonwealth benefits covered about 63 percent of medical charges in an average year, leaving 37 percent to be paid for out-of-pocket (Dewdney, 1972, p.43). The problem was that, whenever the Commonwealth raised its benefits, doctors raised their fees correspondingly (Kewley, 1965, pp.363-365). Efforts to stop this were invariably not successful, even when the Australian Medical Association agreed to exert a constraining influence. One relatively unsuccessful effort in 1965 was later assessed by the president of the Sydney Eastern Suburbs Medical Association as a policy "conceived in haste, born in confusion and (possessed of) a precarious infancy" (ibid., p.365).

The weaknesses of the voluntary health insurance approach were well known by the mid-1960's, at least by health economists and analysts. Thus when the government established a committee of inquiry into health insurance in 1969, its findings were not surprising. The Nimmo Report (so named because the committee was chaired by Mr Justice J.A. Nimmo) identified seven major weaknesses, which are reproduced verbatim below:

1. The operation of the health insurance scheme is unnecessarily complex and beyond the comprehension of many.

2. The benefits received by contributors are frequently much less than the cost of hospital and medical treatment.

3. The contributions have increased to such an extent that they are beyond the capacity of some members of the community and involve considerable hardship for others.

4. The rules of many registered organizations including the so-called "special accounts" rules permit disallowance or reduction of claims for particular conditions. The application of these rules has caused serious and widespread hardship.

5. An unduly high proportion of the contributions received by some organizations is absorbed in operating expenses.

6. The level of reserves held by some organizations is unnecessarily high.

7. The cost of illness may include, in addition to hospital accommodation and treatment and medical services a wide range of other services which have never been covered by the health insurance scheme (Committee of Inquiry into Health Insurance, 1969, p.45).

The Nimmo Report made 42 recommendations on how these weaknesses might be resolved. The publication of these recommendations was followed by the establishment of a Senate Select Committee on Medical and Hospital Costs, which was designed to review the matter at the political level. The Senate's finding, published in June, 1970, did little more than reiterate the Nimmo Report's recommendations. Finally, the National Health Act was revised and a new Health Benefits Plan was introduced on July 1, 1970.

While the new Health Benefits Plan was designed in principle to alleviate all of the weaknesses identified by the Nimmo Report, the major purpose in practice was to deal with the criticism that voluntary health insurance gave most patients inadequate coverage. Concerning medical services, of course, the basic problem was how to get doctors to charge according to a standard schedule of fees rather than in relation to the amount of insurance. The government's solution to the problem was to define insurance benefits in relation to a schedule of most common fees, as ratified by the Australian Medical Association. The AMA, in return, agreed to encourage practitioners to abide by these fees. Upon implementation, the system was designed such that a patient's out-of-pocket expense would be 80 cents for a surgery consultation and $1.20 for a home visit, when provided by a general practitioner. For more costly services, the specified patient cost increased proportionately up to a maximum of $5 for a service costing $40 or more (Dewdney, 1972, p.70).

The "most common fee" approach did not work well, even though it received support from the Australian Medical Association. Most doctors saw the approach as an abrogation of their right to price. And general practitioners saw the differential benefit scales as an insinuation that they were second-class doctors. Consequently, on the first day of the Plan's operation, many doctors immediately raised their prices above the agreed upon fees.

While it was easier to deal with voluntary health insurance coverage deficiencies as they related to hospital services than as they related to medical services, the government did little in this area. Its main action was to provide a new Commonwealth payment of $2 per day direct to hospitals in respect of patients (other than those in the Pensioner Medical Service) treated free of charge. This action allowed states and hospitals to adopt more lenient attitudes in their definitions of charity patients. The main financial beneficiary of the policy was Queensland, with its already existing free public bed hospital service.

Prior to the new Health Benefits Plan, the government in October of 1969 had responded to an implied criticism of the Nimmo Report, that voluntary health insurance left uninsured those people who needed help the most. Arrangements were made to provide free health insurance for persons receiving unemployment, sickness or special benefits under the Social Services Act; for migrants during their first two months in Australia; and for families with weekly incomes not exceeding $39. By the time the new Health Benefits Plan was introduced, the maximum weekly income determining free insurance had been raised to $42.50. There was also partial help for families earning more than this. Families earning more than $42.50 but less than $45.50 could have two-thirds of their insurance premiums paid for by the government, while families earning between $45.50 and $48.50 were eligible for a subsidy of one-third. This scheme became known as the Subsidised Health Benefits Plan.

The government also responded to the criticism that "special account" contributors often received discriminatory and inadequate insurance coverage. Under the new Health Benefits Plan, the Commonwealth government guaranteed payments in respect of special account subscribers so that they could receive the same benefits as regular subscribers.

Finally, the government attempted to respond to criticisms about the excessive complexity of insurance organization offerings, with their associated high administrative costs. Each insurer was restricted to operating one open fund in each state, registration of the fund being conditional on it being expected to be efficient and economic (ibid., p.75).

[73]

Medibank: 1972-1976

The Liberal/National Country Party government's "band-aid" approach to its voluntary health insurance system increased its complexity, but did little to resolve its basic weaknesses. The system was therefore due for review when the Australian Labor Party, which was still committed to national health insurance, won the December, 1972, election. The Labor Party's plan, which had been set out in some detail during the election campaign, involved the following features:

1. The establishment of a single Health Insurance Fund to finance medical and hospital benefits to which the whole population was entitled.

2. Medical coverage, based on benefits calculated at 85 percent of the fees in a schedule negotiated with representatives of the medical profession. The maximum difference between fees and benefits was $5 for any one service. Doctors could bill the plan direct, in bulk, and accept the benefits in full settlement, or bill their patients with the benefit then payable to the patient.

3. Free hospital treatment in standard ward accommodation, without means test, under agreements negotiated with the states. Treatment included medical care provided by doctors appointed by the hospital. Outpatient treatment was also available without means test and without charge. Doctors providing services to "hospital" patients were to be remunerated by salaries and sessional payments. Public hospitals continued to admit private patients, at fees agreed between the governments, and preferred accommodation was available.

4. Funding of the Health Insurance Fund by a 1.35 percent levy on taxable incomes with a matching Commonwealth government subsidy (Deeble, 1982, p.715).

While the Labor Party believed that a major strength of its plan was its political viability, phasing it in after coming into power proved to be no easy task. It took three years, over which time the government faced obstructions from the medical profession, the private insurers, and the Liberal/National Country Party opposition (which retained control over the Senate). The main obstruction from the medical profession was predictable. Doctors did everything possible to make sure that government policies did not lead to fees being constrained by medical insurance. A pattern developed whereby a schedule of fees agreeable to the AMA would be set up, and then most practitioners would disregard it (Scotton, 1978, p.116). Their actions led to fee increases of 15 percent in 1973-74, 20 percent in 1974-75, and 25 percent in 1975-76, the first and only year of Medibank (Deeble and Scotton, 1977, p.346). These increases made the government's policies simultaneously expensive and ineffective.

The obstructions which the Labor Party faced in dealing with private health funds were fostered in large measure by the partisan decisions of the Senate. When legislation was presented in 1974 to enable the government to control fund contribution rates, as a way of smoothly phasing in the public system, the legislation was amended by the Senate to allow judicial appeals. The major New South Wales funds immediately launched an appeal, in which they were successful. When Medibank was eventually introduced, on July 1, 1975, the government was also forced to allow private insurers the right to offer supplementary insurance above the level of public benefits. This effectively eliminated the major mechanism which the government had for constraining medical fees.

The Senate frustrated the government's policies in ways other than by supporting the private insurers. The Health Insurance Bill creating Medibank, which was introduced into parliament in November, 1973, did not become law until August, 1974, because of Senate obstructions. The Senate rejected the Bill on two different occasions, and forced the government to a double dissolution of the two houses of parliament, followed by a joint sitting of both houses, before the Bill was eventually passed. Senate opposition proved sufficient to keep the Medibank funding legislation from ever being passed. The Health Insurance Levy Bill, and the Health Insurance Levy Assessment Bill - alternative attempts by the government to introduce a tax of 1.35 percent of taxable income as a Medibank levy - never became law. Consequently, Medibank had to be completely financed from existing taxation - an arrangement which over time contributed perversely to a view that the Labor government was fiscally irresponsible.

Despite all the problems, Medibank eventually became operational on July 1, 1975. When it was initially implemented, the hospital insurance component was available only in the Territories, South Australia and Tasmania. However, Commonwealth hospital agreements with the remaining states were implemented relatively quickly - Victoria and Western Australia on August 1, Queensland on September 1, and New South Wales on October 1, 1975.

Under Medibank, patients who had traditionally been treated under the Pensioner Medical Service, the special trust accounts, and the Subsidized Health Benefits Plan were no longer treated differently in an institutional sense from the rest of the population. When receiving hospital care, they tended to be public bed patients. And when receiving medical services, doctors accepted the 85 percent of the scheduled fees as full payment, bulk billing the government on their behalf. Administratively, Medibank simplified Australia's health insurance system considerably.

Unfortunately, Medibank was in place for only a very short period before the Labor government was defeated at the polls in December, 1975. The consequence was a dismantlement of Medibank before an empirical assessment of its financial strengths and weaknesses could be made.

Retrenchment: 1976 to Present

Although the incoming Liberal/National Country Party government was pledged to maintain Medibank, it left the system in its original form only until October, 1976, before implementing "reforms". The initial reforms were designed mainly to put Medibank on a sound financial basis - something which the government had prevented while it had been in opposition. For financial purposes, a health insurance levy of 2.5 percent of taxable income was levied, with a maximum amount applying at just under the average earnings figure for all Australians. This feature of the government's reforms was, of course, comparable to the previous Labor government's plan. But it varied from the Labor government's plan in giving citizens the right to opt out of the levy, by providing evidence of subscription to a private fund with benefits equal to the public arrangements. According to Scotton, the financial characteristics of this option guaranteed the high income half of the market for private insurers (Scotton, 1980, pp.180-181). [26]

The government's "reforms" effectively reintroduced private insurance, in line with the private insurers' wishes. In view of this, the role of the public insuring agency had to be modified somewhat. It was renamed Medibank Private and, in addition to providing the tax financed public insurance, was authorized to sell all types of health insurance in competition with the private insurers.

The government's efforts to constrain its financial commitment to health care resulted not only in it shifting much of the insurance from the public agency to the private insurers but also in it modifying the set of hospital agreements with the states that had been set up by the Labor government. These agreements bound the Commonwealth government to meet 50 percent of the state public hospital operating costs. In May, 1976, Prime Minister Malcolm Fraser declared these agreements invalid, on the basis that they did

---

[26]

According to Scotton:

> "Consumers had three options: (1) to pay the levy (if liable) and qualify for Standard Medibank benefits only; (2) to pay the levy (if liable) and purchase supplementary private insurance to meet hospital fees charged to private patients, or (3) to opt out and purchase combined hospital and medical insurance .... options (1) and (2) were available under the original Medibank program .... although the cheapest option at any level of income was to retain Medibank-only coverage, this was not the most economic option for people on higher incomes who valued the additional benefits from private insurance .... at incomes up to these amounts ($8600 for families and $4300 for single persons) it would have cost less to remain in Medibank and purchase supplementary hospital insurance. Above these crossover points it cost less to opt out".

not conform to the <u>Hospital Insurance Act</u>. New agreements were drawn up whereby the Commonwealth paid 50 percent of "approved" net operating costs. From subsequent actions, it became clear that the Commonwealth unilaterally decided what "approved' meant. In 1977, the state governments found their hospital grants arbitrarily reduced by 5 percent, without prior notice from the Commonwealth government. Not surprisingly, actions like this initiated a period of extremely severe budget constraints as far as public hospitals were concerned (ibid., p.185).

The "reforms" initiated by the government in 1976 resulted in a health insurance system which was still compulsory, but which was semi-private as to funding. The system became known as Medibank Mark II, and remained in place until October, 1978. At that time, changes were introduced which effectively phased out national health insurance for medical services. The health insurance levy, the notion of a standard insurance arrangement to which all Australians must insure, and opting out, were all abolished. In their place, the government instituted a new universal medical benefit arrangement, involving benefits equal to 40 percent of schedule fees, with a maximum $20 gap between the benefit and the scheduled fee for any item. The benefits were payable from the government to patients, upon submission of receipts.

While the new arrangement was probably to the financial benefit of most middle and high income persons, it implied substantial hardships for the poor and disadvantaged. Consequently, the government was forced to reintroduce programs comparable to the Pensioner Medical Service and the Subsidized Health Benefits Plan, which had ceased in 1975. For pensioners and their dependants, the government decided to pay 85 percent of scheduled fees, with a maximum patient payment per service of $5. For "socially disadvantaged persons", the government decided to pay 75 percent of scheduled fees, but without any arrangement for a maximum gap. In addition, doctors who were prepared to accept the above payments as payments in full continued to be allowed to bulk bill the government (ibid., pp.209-210).

The 1978 health insurance changes had an effect on the health funds which the government did not anticipate. It largely removed the need for middle and high income individuals to insure privately. For medical care, a maximum per service charge of $20 (provided that doctors charged the scheduled fees) was not an excessive risk to take. And since the hospital agreements were still in operation, all Australians were still entitled to free public bed hospital care. The consequence was that many Australians allowed their private health insurance to lapse, causing the health funds financial difficulties. To resolve these difficulties, the government, in November, 1979, replaced the 40 percent benefit arrangement with a government subsidy equal to the excess over $20 per service up to the schedule fee, payable through the private funds (Deeble, 1982, p.717). This change forced Australians to insure privately, if they wished to benefit from the government's subsidies for medical services.

The government's 1978 and 1979 legislation effectively phased out the national health insurance concept in respect to medical services, but left it intact for hospital care. It was more or less inevitable that the same kind of phasing out procedure would eventually also be applied to the hospital sector. In September, 1981, the government did not renew its public hospital pseudo cost sharing funding agreements with the states (except in South Australia and Tasmania, where they did not expire until 1985). The agreements were replaced by a system of general revenue grants (so-called identified health grants). While these grants were unconditional, and the government stated at the time of their implementation that henceforth responsibility for hospital financing policy would revert to the states, it is of note that the transfer amounts were defined on the explicit assumption that the states would (1) re-institute both inpatient and outpatient charges at specified rates, and (2) restrict free public bed hospital care to pensioners, recent migrants, the unemployed, and low income earners qualifying under a federally administered means test. Only Queensland, with its long tradition of a free hospital service, was in a position to resist the Commonwealth pressure to re-introduce charges for public beds.

While the major policy changes in September, 1981, related to the hospital grants, there were some minor changes in respect of medical services. The general medical benefit payable through the private health funds, and specified in 1979 as an amount equal to the excess over $20 per service up to the schedule fee, was changed to 30 percent of the schedule fee. For pensioners, the unemployed and migrants, however, the decision was made, in each case, to pay 85 percent of schedule fees.

Finally, in September, 1981, the tax deductibility of private health insurance premiums was restored - a tax deduction which had been allowed to lapse in 1976. This change, along with all of the others which had been made by the Liberal/National Country Party government since 1976, brought health financing in Australia basically full circle after a period of about a decade. By late 1981, the system of subsidized voluntary health insurance had been completely re-instituted, with special arrangements for those considered to be poor and disadvantaged.

Australia's Current Financing Arrangement

In view of the government's policy of dismantling Medibank, it is interesting to see how this is reflected in the financial statistics. Unfortunately, the available data are sufficiently sparse and out of date that it is difficult to get a quantitative perspective of the magnitudes involved. Table 4-1 provides a rough picture of the sources of health care funding in 1970-71, when the voluntary subsidized health insurance arrangement was in place, in 1975-76, when Medibank was in place, and in 1978-79, when Medibank was in the early stages of dismantlement.

Table 4-1: Sources of Funding for Public Hospitals and for Medical Services in Australia, 1970-79

Source	Public Hospitals			Medical Services		
	1970-71 (%)	1975-76 (%)	1978-79 (%)	1970-71 (%)	1975-76 (%)	1978-79 (%)
Public Finance	81.66	87.37	80.89	44.63	85.00	44.24
Commonwealth	21.30	45.06	42.34	44.63	85.00	44.24
State	60.36	42.31	38.55	0.00	0.00	0.00
Private Finance	18.34	12.63	19.11	55.38	15.00	55.76
Insurance	10.64	n.a.	12.52	22.70	0.00	37.82
Other	7.70	n.a.	6.59	32.67	15.00	16.94
Total	100.00	100.00	100.00	100.00	100.00	100.00

Sources: (1) Brown (1977)

(2) Commonwealth Department of Health (1981)

(3) Palmer (1982)

For public hospitals, the impact of Medibank was to increase the public funding by about 5 percent (from 82 percent to 87 percent), and to decrease private funding by the same amount. The change was relatively small, indicating that under voluntary insurance in 1970-71 the public hospital sector was already heavily subsidized. The more substantial change was in the proportion of public funding coming from the Commonwealth, as opposed to the state governments. The Commonwealth's share rose from approximately one-third in 1970-71 to approximately one-half in 1975-76, reflecting the effect of changing from per diem to cost sharing hospital grants.

From 1975-76 to 1978-79, the major change in hospital funding was a decrease in the proportion of the funds coming from governments of about 6 percent. This reflected the shift from Medibank I to Medibank II, which induced the high income half of the population to opt out of the public insurance arrangement. Over this period, there was only a minor change in the proportions of public funds coming from the Commonwealth and state governments. However, this was to be expected since the hospital agreements affecting the proportions were left more or less unchanged until late in 1981.

For medical services, the impact of Medibank was to increase public funding from about 45 percent to about 85 percent, all of which came from the Commonwealth government. The dismantlement of Medibank, to the extent that it occurred between 1975-76 and 1978-79, both induced more private expenditures in place of government finance and induced more private insurance to meet the increased private costs. The nature of the changes between 1978-79 and 1981-82 would lead one to expect a further extrapolation of these trends, although the data are not yet available to make estimates of their precise magnitudes.

After September, 1981, the basic health insurance arrangement available to Australians not eligible for one of the special arrangements offered to the old and poor had the following characteristics. The plan covered 85 percent of doctors' scheduled fees, leaving patients with 15 percent of the cost up to a maximum charge of $10 per service (where the scheduled fee was adhered to). Of the 85 percent, 30 percent represented a benefit from the Commonwealth government and 55 percent represented a benefit from the private insurer. For hospital services, the plan covered up to $105 per day for inpatient hospital accommodation, up to $24 for each outpatient treatment involving a medical service, up to $12 for each outpatient treatment not involving a medical service, and up to $55 per day for same day in-hospital treatment. In the case of fund members choosing to be treated as public patients in public hospitals, an extra benefit up to $48 per day was available for services provided by salaried doctors. In the case of fund members choosing to go to private hospitals, a direct Commonwealth subsidy of $16 per day was available (which was increased to $28 when certain prescribed surgical procedures were performed). This package of benefits had an approximate cost of $310 annually for single subscribers, and $620 for families.

It should be noted that, while the hospital benefits in the above package were substantial, they by no means covered all hospital costs. A substantial proportion of public hospital costs continued to be met by state governments, with all remaining costs met by patients.

CHAPTER 5

PUBLIC POLICY AND NATIONAL HEALTH INSURANCE

In Chapter 1, some of the available evidence suggesting that a
national health insurance system is more efficient than a private
arrangement was provided. The comparative financial data on Canada
and Australia support this hypothesis. Consider the material in
Table 5-1. At the beginning of the 1970's, Canada was allocating a
higher proportion of its GNP to hospital and medical services than
was Australia. In 1972-1973, Canada allocated approximately 4.65
percent of its national output to these services while Australia
allocated 3.89 percent. This was partly because Canada had a higher
per capita income than Australia, and the income elasticity of demand
for health care exceeds unity. [27] But more significantly, it was the
period when Canada had just completed phasing in national health
insurance - a process which had caused health care expenditures to
increase rapidly.

From 1972 to 1976, Canada's health insurance arrangement remained
unchanged while Australia's was in a state of flux. This led to costs
increasing more rapidly in the latter country than in the former. By
1975-76, Australia was allocating 5.02 percent of its GNP to hospital
and medical services, while Canada was allocating 4.69 percent
(Table 5-1).

As noted in Chapter 4, the high cost of Medibank was one of the
justifications that the Liberal/National Country Party government
had for dismantling it. The dismantlement did not reduce costs,
however. Australia's hospital and medical costs continued to
increase, accounting for 5.30 percent of GNP in 1978-79, compared

---

27

  Newhouse (1977) has estimated that the inter-country per capita
income elasticity of demand for health care is 1.31.

Table 5-1: Expenditures on Institutional Care and on Medical Services as a Proportion of Gross Domestic Product in Australia and as a Proportion of Gross National Product in Canada, 1972-79

Year	Institutional Care		Medical Care		Total	
	Australia (%)	Canada (%)	Australia (%)	Canada (%)	Australia (%)	Canada (%)
1972-73	2.91	3.21	0.97	1.44	3.89	4.65
1974-75	3.51	3.19	0.92	1.33	4.43	4.52
1975-76	3.85	3.27	1.17	1.42	5.02	4.69
1978-79	4.07	3.19	1.23	1.51	5.30	4.70

Sources: (1) Deeble (1978)

(2) Grant and Lapsley (1981)

(3) Statistics Canada, Catalogue 68-207, various issues

Notes: (1) In both countries, institutional expenditures include capital outlays as well as current expenditures on general hospitals, chronic hospitals, convalescent hospitals, isolation hospitals and mental hospitals. In Australia, they also include expenditures on nursing homes. In Canada, the expenditures are constrained to public expenditures, but for all practical intents and purposes this is equivalent to total expenditures. Finally, in Australia, institutional expenditures include outpatient hospital costs while in Canada they do not.

(2) In Australia, medical care expenditures include all expenditures on medical services provided by private practitioners and businesses. In Canada, medical care expenditures include all public expenditures on general physician services, dental and visiting nurse services, drugs, and hospital outpatient care services.

with 4.70 percent in Canada. If the Australian government had been really interested in cost containment, then it would have devoted its efforts to phasing in Medibank efficiently rather than to dismantling it. But political and ideological considerations loomed large in the government's health policy decisions.

In Chapter 1, it was also suggested that the analysis of the determinants of the Medibank dismantlement provided a convenient focus for the monograph. From the beginning, of course, the reason for Medibank's dismantlement was obvious at a superficial level. It was dismantled because a government hostile to it was elected before it had become politically entrenched. The objective of the monograph was not to establish this but to learn more about the relatively complex set of socio-economic forces underlying political decisions, not only as they have related to Medibank but also as they related to health financing policies in general.

The Episodic Nature of Social Policy Evolution

The analysis of public policy suggests that some periods are more propitious than others for the implementation and maintenance of social programs. In the past, the decades of the 1910's, the 1940's and the 1960's were relatively favourable; while the decades of the 1920's, the 1930's, the 1950's and the 1970's were not. The pattern suggests that favourable periods occur when (1) there is scepticism about the efficacy of the market economy, (2) there is confidence in the efficacy of social planning, or (3) there is sufficient affluence that social programs can be easily financed.

The relation between the state of the economy and social programs is more complex than the above statement indicates, however. While it is true that affluence makes social programs more affordable it is also true that it makes many of them less necessary. The countervailing effects make it impossible to define an empirical relationship on a priori grounds. As if this is not enough, the relation is further complicated by the fact that social programs are sometimes viewed as solutions to recessionary conditions, and at other times as determinants of them.

In this regard, a comparison of the 1930's with the late 1970's is instructive. Measured in terms of unemployment rates and falls in real GNP, the Depression of the 1930's was far worse than the recession of the 1970's. But during the 1930's, policy makers lost their faith in the optimality of the unfettered market economy, and replaced it with Keynesian interventionism. [28] During the 1970's, policymakers came to be attracted to monetarism and "Reaganomics".[29] The shift in ideological views influenced public policy. During the Great Depression, governments typically started out with extremely small social programs, but expanded them when it was financially manageable. During the 1970's recession, they inherited large social programs but dismantled them when it was politically feasible.

In this context, it is possible to view both the electoral defeat of the Australian Labor Party in 1975 and the dismantlement of Medibank from 1976 to 1982, as partly the result of a backlash against Keynesian interventionist liberalism in favour of "laissez-faire" conservatism.

---

[28]
   It is of note that many policymakers started employing Keynesian-type policies even before Keynes' book was published.

[29]
   Many adherents of "Reaganomics", who are common not only in the USA but also elsewhere, attribute the lack of growth of the late 1970's, not to rapidly rising energy prices and recessionary phases of the business cycle, but to laziness of the poor and unemployed. The dismantling of social programs - particularly relating to unemployment insurance and social welfare - is thus justified as a means of restoring growth, by inducing people to look harder for jobs, and to work harder when they get them. But if dismantling social programs has the ultimate effect of restoring growth, it has the immediate effect of constraining taxes - a policy pressed for by middle and high income individuals whose real incomes are no longer increasing.

The Constant Nature of Medical Profession Politics

If conditions conducive to social programs vary over time, the medical profession's reaction to them does not. During most periods and in most countries, doctors have always maintained their support for the principle of professional control over medical markets. For patients with the ability to pay, this has meant that doctors must have the right to price as they see fit. For patients without the ability to pay, government subsidization has been perceived as being appropriate, but not in any way that interferes with the doctor's autonomy with respect to pricing and with respect to his ability to select patients.

The above principle does not imply a necessity for medical services being priced on a fee-for-service basis, except insofar as this represents doctors' preferences. Most doctors in fact have preferred this method of payment. However, this has not reflected any clinical consideration, but rather that under most economic conditions fee-for-service is conducive to larger profits.

It is important to realize that fee-for-service is not a natural outcome of a competitive market arrangement, as doctors are wont to argue. If medical services were provided competitively, as many pricing procedures would exist as sellers and buyers have the ingenuity to devise. Not only fee-for-service, but also capitation, salary, hourly charges, and all other pricing methods would develop up to the limit of their comparative advantages. Restricting the method of payment to fee-for-service is not a simulation of competitive market results but a destruction of them. It means not only that fee-for-service must be used in instances where it is not the most economical means of payment (as in hospitals) but also that fee-for-service will function inefficiently even in circumstances where it would normally have a comparative advantage. Consider the deplorable state of fee-for-service in North America. The fee schedules have become so detailed and so complex that they are meaningless to patients - and, on occasion, not all that meaningful to doctors. Moreover, they promote different degrees of profitability, in particular favouring surgical services over pharmaceutical care. Both developments are inconsistent with an efficient pricing mechanism, and would not have developed in the fee-for-service procedure if there had been meaningful competition. If, for example, a significant proportion of doctors had traditionally adopted the procedure of billing by means of hourly consulting fees, then doctors preferring fee-for-service would have been forced to define prices in terms meaningful to patients. Efforts to obfuscate by creating complex schedules would have resulted in a loss of customers to the doctors imposing hourly charges. Moreover, it would not have been possible for fee-for-service doctors to earn more for some services than for others. Patients would refuse to come for the services that were priced excessively.

In the same way that doctors' support for the principle of professional autonomy does not necessarily mean fee-for-service, it does not necessarily mean full reliance on private health insurance. Doctors normally prefer private insurance because private insurers can be relied upon to be passive partners in the pricing process. But they are fully aware of the economic advantages from public insurance, particularly in the provision of services to low income people.

The evidence gleaned from all countries considered - Canada, Australia, Britain and the United States - suggests that most medical behaviour is economically rather than altruistically motivated. This shatters the illusion of most patients, who like to think that their doctors place human welfare above financial considerations. But shattered the illusion must be, if governments are ever to get electoral support for policies designed to increase the economic efficiency of health care markets. These policies include national health insurance, if a society is committed to the significant subsidization of health care user charges.

It is ironic that the medical profession opposes national health insurance in both Canada and Australia because of bureaucratic inefficiencies, and because of governments becoming "the monopoly buyers and sellers of all medical services" (Saskatchewan Medical Association, 1962). These are exactly the problems generated by physician self-regulation. Only then the problems are professional bureaucratic inefficiencies and private monopoly, while the individuals suffering are patients.

The Role of Government

In principle, the role of government in a democratic society is easy to define. Its function is to implement and maintain public policies, including social programs, which are preferred by a majority of the population. On this basis, there is a strong case for national health insurance in both Canada and Australia, but if this view is doubted it is always possible to resort to plebiscites.

When societies opt for national health insurance, they are opting for a relatively efficient social policy. But even if inefficient policies were opted for, it would be the responsibility of governments to implement them. The only ethical recourse which policymakers have in the latter situation is to inform people about the adverse features of the programs being selected - which, needless to say, does not include propaganda.

The problem with defining optimal public policy in principle is that it is not clear how it can be reconciled with the constraints facing governments in practice. The problem of dealing with politically powerful pressure groups that want policies in opposition to the public interest is particularly difficult. While it is unethical to capitulate to such groups, it is imprudent to ignore them. The evidence in this study suggests three procedures which are helpful in such circumstances. De facto, they can be considered as guidelines for integrating principle with practice, for governments that are inclined to do so.

In considering these guidelines and the evidence suggesting them, it is important to realize that the major politically established programs are not national health insurance in Canada and Medibank in Australia, but national health insurance in Canada and voluntary health insurance in Australia. Established programs are identified, not through their goals or their methods of operation, but through their longevity and through their resistance to dismantlement.

The first guideline is to phase in a desired program relatively slowly. This is a particularly important rule when substantial financial ramifications are involved. It gives the public time to become acquainted with program results, and it gives them time to adjust their budgets accordingly.

Both Canada's national health insurance and Australia's voluntary insurance had long phasing in periods. Consider first the Canadian implementation. Canadians were initially familiarized with the benefits and costs of public hospital insurance during the late 1940's through the introduction of programs in Saskatchewan and British Columbia. They were thus reasonably well acquainted with them by the mid-1950's when they were proposed at the national level. A similar time frame existed for medical insurance, although in this case there were two implementation stages rather than one. Saskatchewan residents were exposed to public medical insurance for about twelve years through the Swift Current program before it was proposed at the provincial level. Then Canadians had about seven or eight years experience with Saskatchewan's plan before it was introduced nationally. The phasing in process was particularly important for medical insurance, because the profession attempted to capitalize on fears that "socialized medicine" would lead to lengthy queues at doctors' offices and to spiralling costs. Australia's voluntary health insurance arrangements also had a long phasing in period, but rather less intentionally than was the case for the Canadian system. The Labor government's efforts to introduce national health insurance from 1941 to 1949 inadvertently provided a backdrop to the Liberal/Country Party government's policies of the early 1950's. It made them appear extremely constrained and financially conservative, although in reality they implied substantial increases in public expenditures on health.

The second guideline is to structure a desired program to get support from as many political pressure groups as possible, when such structuring does not seriously compromise the objectives in mind. The theoretical basis for this guideline is apparent. The more political support that a program has, the less sensitive it is to changes in electoral or economic conditions.

In considering the evidence concerning the second guideline, it is important to note that there are at least six major pressure groups in relation to health. Most obviously, there are the medical associations. But there are also the hospital administrations and the insurance agencies, which, like the doctors, see health from the supply side. From the demand side, there are the consumer organizations. There are also organizations like the Chambers of Commerce which, when they do lobby, do so on behalf of high income individuals. Finally, there are the provincial or state governments, which often function as political lobbyists in relation to national policies.

As mentioned in Chapter 1, Canadian national health insurance had only one major objective, and that was to eliminate health care user charges. Within this constraint, it made every effort to appeal to most of the political pressure groups. The decision to retain fee-for-service and consumer choice of doctor appealed both to high income patients and to doctors. The decision to leave hospitals with their original patterns of ownership and management, and to allow doctors with "access rights" to continue to run hospitals as professional co-operatives, also appealed to doctors, as well as to hospital administrators. Finally, the decision to decentralize the constitutional and administrative control of the programs appealed to the provincial governments.

The major group which Canadian national health insurance made no effort to appease was the insurance companies. Instead, the system was introduced in such a way that opposition from this quarter was thwarted. Public hospital insurance was initially introduced separately from public medical insurance, forcing the medical profession to choose between supporting the insurance companies (which opposed it) and the hospital associations (which favoured it). They opted for the latter, which meant that when public medical insurance was eventually proposed, the insurance companies were no longer available as allies.

The Australian introduction of voluntary health insurance during the 1950's was a masterpiece in meeting the demands of political pressure groups. By subsidizing the cost of health services it appealed to consumers, and by subsidizing through voluntary plans, it appealed particularly to high income consumers. It also appealed to the health insurance funds and to the doctors. The funds were pleased, not only because they retained a major portion of the health insurance markets, but also because these markets were made more buoyant through the subsidies. The doctors were pleased because they retained complete control over fees in a system where patients were made relatively insensitive to prices.

The introduction of Medibank, in contrast to the introduction of voluntary health insurance, was not widely supported politically. Although consumer groups valued it, their support was moderate because of the considerable subsidization of the earlier system. Doctors, health funds and some state governments, on the other hand, actively opposed it. The opposition from the state governments was interesting, because it was something that Canadian medicare had been largely able to avoid. The opposition developed in part because the Australian Labor Party had an organic, rather than a co-operative, view of federalism, which irritated the states. [30] It also developed because of personal incompatibilities between some national and state politicians. In any event, the generation of the hostility of three powerful political groups was not a preferred way of introducing a new program, other things being equal.

The third and final guideline is to rely on economic inducement rather than fiat when this is possible. The advantages of inducement over compulsion are that it generally upsets individuals and organizations less, and gives them less scope for obstructionist behaviour if dissatisfied. Despite the advantages, most governments appear reticent to employ economic inducement policies, relying on them primarily when fiat has been ruled out. Thus they are most common in the area of intergovernmental relations, because constitutional considerations place definite constraints on legislative powers. This issue is discussed in the next section. Here, one might simply note two examples of inducement policies involving the private sector. In Canada, there are the policies relating to extra billing. When provincial governments were precluded from constraining medical fees by fiat, they introduced a number of procedures designed to lower the profitability of doctors charging more than public payments. Despite the timidity of governments in exploiting the potential of these procedures, they worked reasonably well, in the early years eliminating extra billing almost entirely. In Australia, there is the policy of voluntary health insurance. By subsidizing private insurance, the government induced rather than compelled health funds to lower premiums vis-à-vis benefits. It was a policy which could have been justified if health care markets had been perfectly competitive. But the

---

30
At the risk of over-simplification, the "organic" view of federalism sees a federal state as having one government with a number of parts. The federal government is envisioned as the "brain" of the system, responsible for policy formation; and the regional governments are the "arms and legs", responsible for the administration of centrally determined programs. The "co-operative" view of federalism sees central and regional governments as separate units, each with policymaking and administrative functions. The responsibility for policies and programs is divided between them according to equity and efficiency criteria, which makes the federation "co-operative" rather than "constitutional". For evidence that the Australian Labor government between 1972 and 1975 perceived federalism in organic terms, see Sawer (1976) particularly pp.318-319.

ability of doctors to control prices, and the inability of health funds to interfere, destroyed much of the logic of the system.

The Impact of Federalism

As mentioned in the preceding section, economic inducement policies are common in intergovernmental relations. In the case of health, the Canadian Government's introduction of national health insurance through cost sharing grant arrangements is the most obvious example. Because these grants encouraged the provincial governments to see health expenditures in terms of 50 cent dollars, it induced them to spend much more on health services. [31] It accounted for all provinces introducing public hospital and medical insurance programs, whatever the philosophies of their governments. It also accounted for provincial governments attempting to constrain extra billing. To them, a dollar of medical costs financed by patients represented a 50 cent loss to the provincial economy, and was thus something to be avoided.

It seems unlikely that the Canadian government could have successfully introduced national health insurance without the aid of the cost sharing grants. The constitution, of course, was a major impediment to a federally controlled plan (such as Australia has for medical services). But putting aside the constitutional constraints, the prognosis for a federally controlled system would

---

[31]
While the federal government's conditional grant system prior to 1977 was often labelled as cost sharing, it is of note that it was a combination of cost sharing and formula funding. Thus, if a provincial government unilaterally spent $1 more on health care, it did not receive 50 cents as was generally believed. For hospital care, the actual amounts were 25.51 cents in Newfoundland, 25.09 cents in Prince Edward Island, 25.85 cents in Nova Scotia, 25.62 cents in New Brunswick, 31.75 cents in Quebec, 34.45 cents in Ontario, 26.13 cents in Manitoba, 25.87 cents in Saskatchewan, 27.07 cents in Alberta, and 27.66 cents in British Columbia (1975 data). The respective amounts for medical care were 0.66, 0.17, 1.61, 0.96, 12.97, 19.83, 1.88, 1.54, 4.05 and 6.34.

However provincial politicians generally did not understand this. Thus, most acted as though they were spending 50 cent dollars and, to the extent that this led to provinces adopting similar policies, the commonality of the behaviour tended to perpetuate the illusion.

have been poor. The fact of the matter is that the federal government, through its cost sharing grants, stiffened the resolve of provincial governments in facing political pressure groups more than is common for any government at any level. But because cost sharing put the provincial governments into politically difficult situations, they became progressively more disenchanted with it over time.

Cost sharing came under attack economically as well as politically, with many people arguing that the funding arrangement induced inefficiency. It was argued that the open-ended nature of cost sharing promoted spiralling, out of control, costs. It was also argued that cost sharing favoured some methods of doing things over others. Specifically, it was felt that the Canadian arrangement promoted hospitals relative to nursing homes, and doctors relative to other health care practitioners.

Neither of the above arguments is persuasive, either theoretically or empirically. The argument about cost sharing being open-ended, for example, is simply wrong. This is not to say that the introduction of cost sharing does not induce more public spending in the short-run. It does - after all, that is its objective. But once the desired public programs have been phased in, the growth rate in public expenditures settles down to a new equilibrium path. A priori, it is not generally possible to say whether the new equilibrium rate will be greater or smaller than the old. In the case of Canadian national health insurance, however, it turned out to be smaller (Table 1-1).

The argument that cost sharing induces inefficiency by favouring some methods of production over others has more to recommend it. However, this is a criticism of the design of specific cost sharing arrangements rather than a criticism of the funding method. Cost sharing can be made sufficiently global that most of the more troublesome substitution effects are avoided. For example, Canada in 1957 could have applied its funding arrangement to hospitals and nursing homes, or perhaps to all health care institutions, if it had wanted to do so. The choice basically depended on empirical considerations. As an empirical postscript, Canada abandoned cost sharing in 1977, and there is no evidence as yet of provincial governments re-allocating funds away from hospitals and physicians to other institutions and health care practitioners.

If the abandonment of cost sharing has not led to greater efficiency in the health care system, it has facilitated provincial governments partly abandoning the principle of national health insurance. Extra billing has been allowed to become more prevalent, and provincial governments have been edging towards the introduction of hospital user charges (Brown, 1980, p.522). The only mechanism that the federal government has for influencing these matters is its periodic negotiations on the established program grants. It is proving to be a relatively ineffectual instrument.

The fact that cost sharing has a lot to recommend it as a policy tool economically does not negate its political shortcomings. It is most viable politically in a federation that is truly co-operative, and unfortunately there are relatively few of them around. Neither Canada nor Australia approximates very closely the co-operative model. In Canada, the political power of the provinces has been expanding rapidly since the mid-1960's. Currently, many provincial governments - and, in particular, those of Quebec and Alberta - are prepared in principle to allocate very few fiscal functions to the national government, and are prepared in practice to accept only those functions that seem unavoidable under any interpretation of the constitution. It is an arrangement which I have been inclined to label constitutional federalism. Under constitutional federalism, cost sharing is rejected because it is a policy tool which allows the federal government to intrude into the constitutional domain of the provinces. If Canada's federation is dominated by centrifugal forces, Australia's tends to be the reverse. An organic perception of federalism appears to dominate, in which the national government is expected to make most of the policy decisions, and the state governments are expected to adopt accommodating policies whenever this is necessary. Under organic federalism, cost sharing is rejected because intergovernmental inducement policies are not perceived to be necessary.

In effect, although Canada and Australian Federalism are quite different, they are both politically conducive to ignoring the potential of cost sharing programs as a policy tool. Whether, in either of these countries, the economic advantages from such programs can prove sufficient to compensate for their political unpopularity is a moot point.

The Prospects for National Health Insurance

It is not inappropriate to end a study of this kind by speculating what the prospects for national health insurance are. For the immediate future, of course, the general economic climate is not favourable. Not only in Canada and Australia but also in many western world countries, the combination of stringent government budgets and scepticism about the desirability of social programs constrain the support for national health insurance.

With respect to national health insurance, Canada is more fortunate than Australia in having a relatively efficient system already in place. But the ability of this system to withstand an increasingly hostile political environment is open to question. Probably the most immediate policy question is what the implications of a Conservative Party win at a future federal election would be. Although the current Liberal Party government has not been all that energetic in supporting medicare, it has at least considered it to be a valuable social program. Many Conservative politicians actually dislike it, and would find policies similar to those adopted by the Fraser government in Australia quite palatable. However, a Conservative government would be in a position to leave medicare entirely in the hands of the provincial governments, if it wanted - and considering the popularity of medicare, this would represent a strategic political stance. If adopted it would result in a situation comparable to the present.

If Australia does not have national health insurance at the present, the prospects for it are good insofar as the country has just elected an Australian Labor Party government. [32] This government is committed to reintroducing a Medibank type of program (with the intention of calling the new program "Medicare"). The interesting question is how it will proceed in this matter. It is my assessment that, if the Labor Party simply tries to reintroduce Medibank as it was in 1975, this will ultimately set up a sequence of events similar to those of 1975-82. Australia does not have the funds to finance such a program at current tax rate levels, and policies of raising taxes will lead to a drop in electoral support for the new government. (Despite this problem, it should be noted that the Labor government, during the 1983 election campaign, suggested that it would partially fund its Medicare program through an income-related levy of one percent of taxable income). In addition, the medical profession and the health funds are too firmly entrenched to be tackled by means of direct political confrontations - which is what Medicare constitutes.

A more promising route for the new government would be to concentrate initially on a national hospital insurance plan, and to proceed by means of cost sharing arrangements with the states. [33] It hardly needs to be pointed out that Canada proceeded in this way, and its objectives were much more modest than those implicit in the

---

32

An Australian Labor Party government, under the leadership of Mr Hawke, was elected on March 5, 1983.

33

In this regard, it needs to be emphasised that I am proposing cost sharing arrangements of the Canadian type, where the state governments control program expenditures, and the federal government agrees to finance a specified percentage of these expenditures provided that certain conditions are met. Such arrangements differ from the usual Australian cost sharing arrangements, where the federal government determines the level of expenditures and specifies matching conditions for the states.

Australian proposal. The Canadian government in 1957 wanted only to publicly insure all hospital costs in the context of a given institutional structure. Medibank in 1975 was designed not only to publicly insure all hospital costs but also to improve hospital operating efficiency through increased use of salaried hospital doctors. While the latter objective was commendable it increased the medical profession's antagonism to Medibank considerably. This antagonism, and consequent obstructionist behaviour, could be anticipated in relation to any attempt to reintroduce a program with the same objectives. Consequently, it would be prudent to get the desired national hospital plan in place, before tackling doctors in their offices.

If a national hospital plan using salaried hospital doctors could be implemented, it is my belief that the issue of public medical insurance could be subsequently easily resolved. It must be realized that, after the implementation of public hospital insurance, the need for public medical insurance would be relatively low – certainly much lower than it was in Canada in the 1960's. In Canada, from 1958 to 1968, the burden of medical costs remained high because there was no comprehensive public bed hospital service involving salaried doctors, and there were no public benefits concerning private medical services. In Australia, national hospital insurance would presumably mean that patients could receive inpatient medical care free and ambulatory medical care on a subsidized basis (assuming that the medical benefits payable under voluntary health insurance would be continued). If the relatively low need for public medical insurance would be conducive to doctors becoming more amenable towards it, a policy of offering subsidized outpatient services through the hospitals in competition with medical practitioner care would soften their stance even more. In effect, national hospital insurance in Australia would have considerable potential for diminishing the market power of the medical profession – which would increase considerably the political feasibility of introducing public medical insurance.

A policy of promoting national hospital insurance in Australia is promising for reasons other than that it weakens the market power of the medical profession. It would be relatively easy to promote because Australia already has a model of a cost-effective and politically viable plan - that of Queensland (Queensland's hospital operating costs per occupied bed day are about two-thirds of those in any other state). It is also promising because it would cost the Commonwealth government very little money (indeed, in the long run, it would undoubtedly reduce costs). The existing hospital grants would simply have to be set up in a different way.

This is not to say that introducing national hospital insurance would be without difficulties. The medical profession would still be able to exert pressure - but in the long run doctors need hospitals as much as hospitals need doctors. Moreover, there may be other difficulties, not immediately apparent. John Deeble has suggested (to me) that, for political reasons, the Labor Party feels compelled to initiate a full-blown national plan, rather than proceed in a gradual and piecemeal way. [34] Russell Mathews has pointed out that cost sharing arrangements of the Canadian sort would probably not be acceptable to an Australian federal government, because they would effectively transfer too much power to the state governments. [35] I hope, however, that these are not compelling reasons for rejecting national hospital insurance and cost shared funding arrangements, out of hand. [36] In the Tinbergen spirit, one might observe that there is always a shortage of policy tools in relation to policy objectives. Rejecting tools increases the probability that some of

---

[34]

John Deeble is presently Head of the Health Economics Research Unit at the Australian National University. During the late 1960's and early 1970's, he, along with Dick Scotton, was a major architect of the national health insurance plan which eventually became Medibank.

[35]

Russell Mathews is Director and Professor of the Centre for Research on Federal Financial Relations at the Australian National University.

the objectives will not be achieved.

The above discussion of prospects is for the immediate future while recessionary forces and antagonism to social programs persist. Eventually, it is expected, the world economy will recover and people will adopt a more sympathetic attitude to social policy. But how long this change will take in coming, and how substantial the shift will be when it comes, is impossible to say.

36
    In the event that cost sharing arrangements of the Canadian sort were employed in Australia, the formula for defining the equalization grants would have to be modified. At the moment, a state's equalization grant from the Commonwealth equals its entitlement (determined by its fiscal capacity) less the amount of certain specific purpose grants. If cost sharing grants were treated in this way, this would eliminate their financial inducement effect (Commonwealth Grants Commission, 1981, pp.43-51).

REFERENCES

Ackerknecht, E.H. (1955) A Short History of Medicine, Ronald Press Company, New York.

Agnew, C.H. (1974) Canadian Hospitals, 1920-1970, A Dramatic Half Century, University of Toronto Press.

Anderson, O.W. (1972) Health Care: Can There be Equity; The United States, Sweden and England, John Wiley and Sons, New York.

Asimov, I. (1965) A Short History of Biology, Thomas Nelson and Sons Limited, London.

Badgley, R. and Wolfe, S. (1967) Doctor's Strike, Macmillan, Toronto.

Bell, J. (1976) "Queensland's Public Hospital System: Some Aspects of Finance and Control", in Roe, J. (ed.) Social Policy in Australia - Some Perspectives, 1901-1975, Cassell, New South Wales, pp.284-294.

Brown, M.C. (1974) "Medicare and the Medical Monopoly", The Canadian Forum, April, pp.5-9.

Brown, M.C. (1977) The Financing of Personal Health Services in New Zealand, Canada and Australia, Centre for Research on Federal Financial Relations, Research Monograph No.20, Australian National University, Canberra.

Brown, M.C. (1979) "The Health Care Crisis in Historical Perspective", Canadian Journal of Public Health, Vol.70, September, pp.300-306.

Brown, M.C. (1980) "The Implications of Established Program Finance for National Health Insurance", Canadian Public Policy, V.6 No.3, pp.521-532.

Brown, M.C. (1982) The Implications of Established Program Financing for Canadian Federalism, A Study Done for the Ontario Economic Council (unpublished), Toronto.

Bunker, J.P. (1970) "Surgical Manpower: A Comparison of Operations and Surgeons in the United States and in England and Wales, New England Journal of Medicine, V.282, pp.135-144.

Canadian Medical Association (1934) Report of the Committee on Economics.

Carson, R.J. (1974) The End of Medicine, John Wiley and Sons, New York.

Clarke, M. (1980) A Short History of Australia, (Second Revised Edition), A Mentor Book, New York.

Committee of Inquiry into Health Insurance (1969) Report (Nimmo Report), Canberra.

Commonwealth Bureau of Census and Statistics (1943) Official Year Book of the Commonwealth of Australia, 1942 and 1943, Canberra.

Commonwealth Department of Health (1978) A Discussion Paper on Paying for Health Care, Hospitals and Health Services Section, AGPS, Canberra.

Commonwealth Department of Health (1981) Annual Report of the Director General of Health, 1980-81, Canberra.

Commonwealth Grants Commission (1981) Report on State Tax Sharing Entitlements 1981: Volume 1 - Main Report, Australian Government Publishing Service, Canberra.

Corbin, M. and Krute, A. (1975) "Some Aspects of Medicare Experience with Group Insurance Plans", Social Security Bulletin, V.38, March, pp.3-11.

Deeble, J.S. (1970) Health Expenditures in Australia, 1960-61 to 1966-67, Ph.D. Thesis, University of Melbourne.

Deeble, J.S. (1978) Health Expenditure in Australia 1960-61 to 1975-76, Research Report No.1, Health Research Project, Australian National University, Canberra.

Deeble, J.S. (1982) "Financing Health Care in a Static Economy", Social Science and Medicine, V.16, pp.713-724.

Deeble, J.S. and Scotton, R.B. (1977) "Health Services and the Medical Profession", in K.A. Tucker (ed.), Economics of the Australian Service Sector, Croom Helm, London.

Dewdney, J.C.H. (1972) Australian Health Services, John Wiley and Sons, Sydney.

Dickey, B. (1976) "The Labor Government and Medical Services in NSW, 1910-1914" in Jill Roe (ed.), Social Policy in Australia - Some Perspectives, 1901-1975, Cassell, New South Wales, pp.60-73.

Dodge, D.A. (1972) "Occupational Wage Differentials, Occupational Licensing, and Returns to Investment in Education: An Exploratory Analysis", in S. Ostrey (ed.), Canadian

<u>Higher Education in the Seventies</u>, Ottawa, Information
Canada, pp.130-165.

Fox, R.C. (1977) "The Medicalization and Demedicalization of
American Society", <u>Daedalus</u>, Winter, pp.9-22.

Gaus, C., Cooper, B. and Hirschman, C. (1976) "Contrasts in HMO and
Fee-For-Service Performance", <u>Social Security Bulletin</u>,
V.39, May.

Gavett, J.W. and Smith, D.B. (1968) "A Comparison of the Hospital
Cost Experience of Three Competing HMO's", <u>Inquiry</u>,
V.15, No.4, December, pp.327-335.

Grant, C. and Lapsley, H.M. (1981) <u>The Australian Health Care System
1981</u>, Australian Studies in Health Service
Administration No.42, School of Health Administration,
University of New South Wales.

Gray, G. (1982) <u>The Termination of Medibank</u>, B.A. Honours
Sub-thesis in Political Science, Australian National
University, (unpublished).

Grove, J.W. (1969) <u>Organized Medicine in Ontario</u>, A Study for the
Committee on the Healing Arts, Ontario.

Heagerty, J. (1928) <u>Four Centuries of Medical History in Canada</u>, V.1,
Macmillan.

Health and Welfare Canada (1961) <u>Expenditures on Personal Health
Care in Canada, 1953-1961</u>, Ottawa.

Health and Welfare Canada (1978) "Figures Released Provisionally,
Pending Preparation of Published Report in Both Official
Languages", Ottawa.

Hetherington, R., Hopkins, C. and Roemer, M. (1975) <u>Health
Insurance Plans: Promise and Performance</u>, Wiley, New
York.

Illich, I. (1975) <u>Medical Nemesis</u>, McClelland and Stewart, Toronto.

Jewson, N.D. (1974) "Medical Knowledge and the Patronage System in
18th Century England", <u>Sociology</u>, V.8.

Kessel, R.A. (1958) "Price Determination in Medicine", <u>Journal of
Law and Economics</u>, V.1, October, pp.20-53.

Kewley, T.H. (1965) <u>Social Security in Australia</u>, University of
Sydney Press, Sydney.

Keynes, J.M. (1936) <u>The General Theory of Employment, Interest and
Money</u>, Harcourt Brace, London.

Lalonde, M. (1974) A New Perspective on the Health of Canadians, a Working Document, Health and Welfare Canada, Ottawa.

LeClair, M. (1975) "The Canadian Health Care System" in S. Andreopoulos (ed.), National Health Insurance - Can We Learn from Canada, John Wiley and Sons, New York.

Lees, D.S. (1966) Economic Consequences of the Professions, Institute of Economic Affairs, London.

Leu, R.E. (1980) "The Relative Efficiency of Health Service Systems: A Cross-Country Study", Second International Conference on Systems Science in Health Care, University of Montreal.

MacDermot, H.E. (1967) One Hundred Years of Medicine in Canada, McClelland and Stewart, Toronto.

Marmor, T.R. (1970) The Politics of Medicare, Routledge and Kegan Paul, London.

National Council of Welfare (1982) Medicare: the Public Good and Private Practice, Ottawa, May.

Newhouse, J.P. (1977) "Medical Care Expenditures: A Cross National Survey", The Journal of Human Resources, V.12, No.1, Winter, pp.115-123.

Northcott, H.C. (1982) "Extra-Billing and Physician Remuneration: A Paradox", Canadian Public Policy, V.8, No.2, Spring, pp.200-206.

Palmer, G. (1982) "Commonwealth/State Fiscal Relationships and the Financing and Provision of Health Services", in P.M. Tatchell (ed.), Economics and Health, 1981: Proceedings of the Third Australian Conference of Health Economists, Australian National University, Canberra.

Pensabene, T.S. (1980) The Rise of the Medical Practitioner in Victoria, Health Research Project, Research Monograph No.2, Australian National University, Canberra.

Queen's Printer (1964) Royal Commission on Health Services, V.1, Ottawa.

Roe, J. (1976a) "Leading the World? 1901-1914", in J. Roe (ed.) Social Policy in Australia - Some Perspectives, 1901-1975, Cassell Australia, New South Wales, pp.3-23.

Roe, J. (1976b) "Never Again? 1939-1949", in J. Roe (ed.) Social Policy in Australia - Some Perspectives, 1901-1975, Cassell Australia, New South Wales, pp.215-227.

Roemer, M. and Dubois, D.M. (1969) "Medical Costs in Relation to the Organization of Ambulatory Care", The New England Journal of Medicine, V.280, No.18, May.

Rogers, D. (1977) "The Challenge of Primary Care", in J. Knowles (ed.), Doing Better and Feeling Worse - Health in the United States, Norton.

Saskatchewan Medical Association (1962) Newsletter, V.2, May 11.

Saward, E., Blank, J. and Lamb, H. (1972) "Some Information Descriptive of a Successfully Operating HMO", DHEW Pub. No. HSM 73-13011.

Sawer, G. (1976) "Tne Whitlam Revolution in Australian Federalism - Promise, Possibilities and Performance", Melbourne University Law Review, V.10, No.3, pp.315-329.

Sax, S. (1972) Medical Care in the Melting Pot, Angus and Robertson, Sydney.

Scotton, R.B. (1978) "Health Services and the Public Sector", in R.B. Scotton and Helen Ferber (ed.) Public Expenditures and Social Policy in Australia: Volume 1 - The Whitlam Years 1972-75, Longman Cheshire, Sydney.

Scotton, R.B. (1980) "Health Insurance: Medibank and After", R.B. Scotton and Helen Ferber (ed.), Public Expenditures and Social Policy in Australia: Volume II - The First Fraser Years, 1976-78, Longman Cheshire, Sydney.

Starr, P. (1977) "Medicine, Economy and Society in Nineteenth Century America", Journal of Social History, V.10, No.4, Summer 1977, pp.588-607.

Statistics Canada (1971) Canada Year Book, 1970-71, Ottawa.

Statistics Canada, Provincial Government Finance - Revenue and Expenditure, Catalogue 68-207, various issues.

Taylor, M. (1978) Health Insurance and Canadian Public Policy, McGill-Queen's University Press, Montreal.

Thomas, L. (1977) "On the Science and Technology of Medicine", Daedalus, Winter.

Trudeau, P.E. (1977) "Established Program Financing: A Proposal Regarding the Major Shared-Cost Programs in the Fields of Health and Post-Secondary Education", in J.P. Meekison (ed.), Canadian Federalism: Myth or Reality, Methuen, Toronto.

Truman, T. (1969) "Political Ideology, Belief, Systems and Parties: The Australian Labor Party", in R. Preston (ed.),

Contemporary Australia - Studies in History, Politics and Economics, Duke University Press.

Urquhart, M.C. and Buckley, K.A.H. (1965) Historical Statistics of Canada, Macmillan, Toronto.

Vayda, E.A. (1973) "A Comparison of Surgical Rates in Canada and England and Wales", New England Journal of Medicine, V.289, pp.1224-1229.

Wood, G.L. (1976) "A Contemporary Advocate of National Insurance", in J. Roe (ed.), Social Policy in Australia, Cassell Australia, New South Wales.